THE

DYER'S INSTRUCTOR.

THE

DYER'S INSTRUCTOR:

COMPRISING PRACTICAL INSTRUCTIONS IN THE

ART OF DYEING SILK, COTTON, WOOL,

AND

WORSTED AND WOOLLEN GOODS,

AS

SINGLE AND TWO-COLORED DAMASKS, MOREENS, CAMLETS, LASTINGS,
SHOT COBOURGS, SILK STRIPED ORLEANS, PLAIN ORLEANS
FROM WHITE AND COLORED WARPS, MERINOS,
WOOLLENS, YARNS, ETC.

CONTAINING

NEARLY EIGHT HUNDRED RECEIPTS.

TO WHICH IS ADDED,

A TREATISE ON THE ART OF PADDING;

AND THE PRINTING OF

SILK WARPS, SKEINS, AND HANDKERCHIEFS, AND THE VARIOUS
MORDANTS AND COLORS FOR THE DIFFERENT STYLES
OF SUCH WORK.

BY DAVID SMITH,

PATTERN DYER.

PHILADELPHIA:
HENRY CAREY BAIRD,
No. 7 HART'S BUILDINGS.
1853.

PHILADELPHIA:
T. K. AND P. G. COLLINS, PRINTERS.

INTRODUCTION.

IN presenting to the Public my second Work on Dyeing, I have endeavored to give concise and clear directions for Dyeing Wool in its raw state, Cotton in the Hank and Warp, and Silk in the Skein, in all the various colors; and also for Dyeing the different fabrics of Piece Goods, as Damasks, single and two colors, Moreens, Camlets, Lastings, Shot Cobourgs, Silk Striped Orleans, Plain Orleans from White and Colored Warps, Merinos, Woollens, Yarns, &c. Also I have appended a concise Treatise on the Art of Padding; and directions for the Printing of Silk Warps, Skeins, and Handkerchiefs, and the various Mordants and Colors for the different styles of such Work. In this department I have been aided by one of the most practical men in the Silk Printing business.

1*

Since the publication of the "PRACTICAL DYER'S GUIDE," I have received numerous applications for receipts for Dyeing Silk, Cotton, and Wool.— As the "DYER'S GUIDE" is particularly applicable to Stuff, Yarn, and Woollen Cloth Dyers, I have collected the Receipts on Cotton, Silk, and Wool Dyeing, from my own resources, (not from obsolete Books on Dyeing,) and from practical men in the trade who have been prompt to aid me in this attempt to impart practical and scientific knowledge to my brethren in the trade. The following work principally comprises Receipts for Dyeing a given quantity of goods, as Wool, Cotton, and Silk, together with other miscellaneous important information.

To communicate instruction by clear and concise Receipts, must be regarded as best calculated to qualify a person for successful operations in practical dyeing; it will save much time, and also expense; and for a learner, must be far superior to reading and studying the complicated and circuitous methods, as detailed in some Treatises on the Art of Dyeing, which demands the greatest simplicity in its explanations and directions, so that a person from reading them may not be bewildered as in a labyrinth of complexity, but proceed at once to dye. I have endeavored to avoid such a method of instruction, and I presume that the following Receipts will meet the wishes of those who are seeking after such knowledge.— Having myself had much experience in dyeing nearly all sorts of Goods, I have given every class of colors and the different shades of the same color, in as great a variety as I could find calculated to be useful.

As some parties have wished to purchase the "Dyer's Guide," *without the Patterns*, it is necessary to say that only a limited number was published, and the edition is fast running out, and that the few copies remaining must be sold *with* Patterns. But I have endeavored to meet their wishes by the publication of the following Work, and, as the price is so low, considering the important information given, it is presumed that it will be serviceable to the Trade, not excepting those who have purchased the " Guide," on account of those Receipts which refer to Silk, Cotton, and Wool Dyeing. D. S.

CONTENTS.

WOOL-DYEING.

SILK-DYEING.

WOOLLEN YARN DYEING.

WOOLLEN YARN DYEING—Continued.

WORSTED YARN DYEING.

29 Grain Crimson
30 Rose
31 Pink
32 Imitation of Indigo Blue
33 Light Brown
34 Claret Brown
35 Snuff Color
36 Full Black
37 Blue Black
38 Fawn Drab
39 Lilac
40 Lavender

41 Light Puce
42 Slate Drab
43 Sage Drab
44 Red Cinnamon Brown
45 Dark Brown
46 Dark Red Brown
47 Grain Scarlet
48 Salmon
49 Sky Blue
50 Saxon Blue
51 Dove Color

WOOLLEN-DYEING.

1 Grain Scarlet
2 Scarlet
3 Scarlet
4 Scarlet
5 Lac Scarlet
6 Scarlet
7 Scarlet
8 Orange
9 Salmon
10 Salmon
11 Grain Rose
12 Gold Color
13 Grain Rose
14 Full Red Crimson
15 Light Rose
16 Rose Color
17 Yellow
18 Full Yellow, or
19 Sky Blue
20 Dove Color
21 Crimson
22 Green
23 Royal Blue
24 Dark Royal Blue
25 Royal Blue
26 Royal Blue
27 Royal Blue

28 Royal Blue, Gold Lists
29 Green
30 Purple
31 Dark Brown
32 Dark Claret Brown
33 Black
34 Peachwood Red
35 Green
36 Chestnut Brown
37 Dark Green
38 Claret Brown
39 Chromed Green
40 Claret
41 Brown Olive
42 Mule Drab
43 Stone Drab
44 Fawn Drab
45 Nut Brown
46 Good Light Claret
47 Good Crimson
48 Good Logwood Blue
49 Logwood Blue
50 Yarn and Woollen Piece Dyeing
51 New mode of Dyeing Logwood Blues
52 Maroon

2

DAMASK-DYEING.

1 Pink and White	22 Orange
2 Pink	23 Sky Blue and White
3 Salmon and White	24 Sky Blue
4 Salmon	25 Saxon Blue and White
5 Rose Color	26 Saxon Blue
6 Rose Color	27 Light Green and White
7 White and Ponque Color	28 Light Green
8 Ponque	29 Middle Green and White
9 Grain Crimson	30 Middle Green
10 Grain Crimson	31 Cinnamon Brown and White
11 Buff and White	32 Cinnamon Brown
12 Buff	33 Light Fawn
13 Straw Color and White	34 Darker Fawn
14 Straw Color	35 Light Silver Drab
15 Yellow and White	36 Darker Silver Drab
16 Yellow	37 Mock Crimson
17 Lac Scarlet and White	38 Sea Green
18 Lac Scarlet	39 Coffee Brown
19 Grain Scarlet and White	40 Black
20 Grain Scarlet	
21 Light Orange and White	

MOREEN-DYEING.

1 Light Sky Blue	20 Full Silver Drab
2 Dark Sky Blue	21 Light Fawn
3 Full Orange	22 Darker Fawn
4 Light Orange	23 Cinnamon Brown
5 Full Grain Scarlet	24 Darker Cinnamon Brown
6 Grain Scarlet	25 Middle Green
7 Light Lac Scarlet	26 Dark Green
8 Full Lac Scarlet	27 Light Green
9 Light Yellow	28 Darker Green
10 Full Yellow	29 Light Saxon Blue
11 Straw Color	30 Dark Saxon Blue
12 Buff	31 Light Red Crimson
13 Light Grain Crimson	32 Full Red Crimson
14 Dark Grain Crimson	33 Light Rose Color
15 Coffee Brown	34 Full Rose Color
16 Sea Green	35 Light Salmon
17 Mock Crimson	36 Full Salmon
18 Black	37 Light Pink
19 Light Silver Drab	38 Full Pink

TWO-COLORED DAMASK-DYEING.

CAMLET-DYEING.

LASTING-DYEING.

SHOT COBOURG DYEING.

SILK STRIPED ORLEANS FROM BLACK, WHITE, AND COLORED WARPS.

COLORED ORLEANS FROM BLACK WARPS.

NATURE AND USE OF DYEWARES—Continued.

EXAMINATION OF WATER BY TESTS, &c.

THE DYERS' INSTRUCTOR.

WOOL-DYEING.

No. 1.

140 lbs. OF WOOL.—FANCY BLOOM.

Boil 1½ hour with 1 pound of Logwood.
1½ lb. of Barwood.
Sadden with 8 ozs. of Alum.

The Alum must be melted before it is thrown upon the wool, and then well stirred in, so as to make it as even as possible. Then boil half an hour longer.

It is better to melt the saddening, whether it be Alum, Copperas, or Blue Vitriol, as by this means it sooner penetrates the body of the wool, and does not leave a deadness in some parts, as is generally the case when the saddening is put on in the crystal state.

3

No. 2.

140 lbs. OF WOOL.—DRAB.

Boil with ¾ lb. of Barwood.
¾ lb. of Logwood.
2 ozs. of Fustic.
Sadden with 8 ozs. of Copperas.
And then spread well out.

No. 3.

140 lbs. OF WOOL.—HEAVY DRAB.

Boil with 8 ozs. of Logwood.
2 lbs. of Barwood.
1 lb. of Fustic.
Sadden with 1 lb. of Copperas.
Spread out.

No. 4.

130 lbs. OF WOOL.—SLATE COLOR.

Boil with 8 ozs. of Logwood.
2½ lbs. of Barwood.
Sadden with 8 ozs. of Alum.
Spread out.

This shade may be dyed by first boiling the wool in 1 lb. of Chrome for about an hour, then wash and fill it up in a separate pan, with about 1 lb. of Logwood, and 8 ozs. of Cudbear.

But as this mode of dyeing Drabs will not stand Milling and Scouring so well as the former, I cannot recommend it, though some wool-dyers follow this receipt.

No. 5.

130 lbs. OF WOOL.—LIGHT GREEN.

Boil one hour with 1 lb. of Chrome and 8 ozs. of Alum. Then run off the Liquor, and wash well in clean water; dye off with 20 lbs. of Fustic and 8 lbs. of Logwood, and then boil to shade required.

By adding more Logwood in the finishing, any shade of Dark Green may be got. When not Yellow enough, add a little more Fustic.

The colors dyed by means of Chroming are very difficult to distinguish from those of fast Indigo colors, and can only be distinguished by a strong Acid: I shall insert a few of them to accommodate those who are not so much acquainted with the nature of Chrome. From this preparation or Mordant almost any shade may be produced, varying from a Light Drab to a Dark Brown, Dark Green, Dark Purple, Dark Claret, or Dark Olive. Peachwood, Logwood, Fustic,

Camwood, Barwood, and Madder will work after it. Peachwood itself will make a good Claret after it, producing a blue shade; but when too Blue, a little Alum will redden it, and will work as solid and even a color as by any other mode of preparation.

———

No. 6.

130 lbs. OF WOOL.—A DARKER SHADE OF GREEN.

Prepare as above with 1 oz. of Chrome.
8 ozs. of Alum.

Boil one hour, then take it out, and let it soak an hour or two, and then fill it up in another water with

12 lbs. of Logwood.
14 lbs. of Fustic.

———

No. 7.

70 lbs. OF WOOL.—LIGHT BLUE.

Prepare with 8 ozs. of Alum.
8 ozs. of Chrome.
Fill up with 8 lbs. of Ground Logwood, or Chipped Logwood boiled up in bags.

No. 8.

200 lbs. OF WOOL.—LOGWOOD BLUE.

Prepare or boil one hour with 1 lb. of Chrome.
4 lbs. of Alum.
1 lb. of Red Argol.
Clean and finish with 35 lbs. of Logwood, and boil
half an hour in the finishing.

This is a good imitation of Indigo, and it will
bear exposure to the atmosphere. I have taken
this receipt from my *Practical Dyers' Guide*. It
has been used by some parties who have purchased the *Guide*, and they state that this Receipt alone is worth the price of the *Guide*.

No. 9.

50 lbs. OF WOOL.—SAGE DRAB.

Prepare as above with 8 ozs. of Chrome.
8 ozs. of Argol.
4 ozs. of Alum.
Finish with 1 lb. of Logwood.
8 ozs. of Fustic.

If not red enough, add a handful of Cudbear,
and boil an hour.

No. 10.

160 lbs. OF WOOL.—BLACK.

Boil one hour with 4 lbs. of Chrome.

4 lbs. of Alum.

2 lbs. of Red Argol.

Finish in a clean vessel with 40 lbs. of Logwood.

4 lbs. of Barwood.

The wood must be well boiled up in bags before the wool is entered, cool down a little, and enter at about 180°, then boil the wool about an hour.

This is a good Black, and on this principle almost all Blacks are dyed, in stuff goods, and cloth, and wool; but some dyers think it is not so durable as other modes of Dyeing Black. Therefore I will now give two or three different modes of dyeing Blacks on wools.

———

No. A.

Another mode is to boil the wool with Camwood (a sufficient quantity for the bloom) for about two hours, then sadden with Copperas, and let it lie in this all night; next morning, boil it in Logwood for about the same time as before, and then sadden again with Copperas.

This mode is preferred by some, being a much

finer Black, and will stand Milling without losing any of its color. By the former mode it assumes a slight green appearance in the Milling, and consequently loses a little of its darkness.

The best Black is that which is dyed with Indigo in the following manner:—

No. B.

First redden with Camwood as before, but without saddening, and then fill up to the shade in the woad vat.

Either Blue Black or full Black may be dyed in this way, and it is certainly the best and firmest mode of dyeing cloth. It will stand exposure to the atmosphere, and resist any acid applied to it for a test, neither fading nor being diminished in any measure; even Sulphuric Acid of double strength will not injure the color, but rather brighten it than otherwise.

This is an expensive mode of dyeing a Black, but it is worth any amount charged for it, on account of its firmness and durability.

No. 11.

140 lbs. OF WOOL.—FAST BLUE BLACK.

Boil with 10 lbs. of Camwood.

3 lbs. of Alum.

2 lbs. of Red Argol.

And leave in the pan all night, then blue up about one-half in the vat, and then in another pan boil it one hour with

40 lbs. of Logwood.

And sadden with 2 lbs. of Copperas.

No. 12.

160 lbs. OF WOOL.—CALIFORNIA COLOR.

Prepare or boil one hour with 2 lbs. of Chrome.

2 lbs. of Red Argol.

2 lbs. of Alum.

Clean and finish in another vessel with 4 lbs. of Camwood.

40 lbs. of Fustic.

30 lbs. of Crop Madder.

If a brighter shade be required, add 1 Gill of Oil of Vitriol.

All the various shades of this color may be dyed after this mode, by increasing or diminishing the same wares, according to shade required.

No. 13.

120 lbs. OF WOOL.—DARKER SHADE OF CALIFORNIA COLOR.

Another mode of dyeing this color is as follows :—

Boil two hours with 20 lbs. of Fustic.
24 lbs. of Crop Madder.
12 lbs. of Camwood.
Sadden with 4 ozs. of Copperas.

No. 14.

66 lbs. OF WOOL.—FAWN DRAB.

Boil with 4 ozs. of Logwood.
1¾ lbs. of Barwood.
Sadden with 8 ozs. of Alum.
Get out when boiled to the shade, and spread.

No. 15.

70 lbs. OF WOOL.—DARK FAWN DRAB.

Boil with 3 lbs. of Barwood.
3½ lbs. of Fustic.
8 ozs. of Logwood.
Sadden with 2 lbs. of Copperas.

No. 16.

170 lbs. OF WOOL.—MADDER DRAB.

Boil with 3½ lbs. of Barwood.
8 lbs. of Fustic.
3 lbs. of Logwood.
Sadden with 1 lb. of Copperas.

———

No. 17.

56 lbs. OF WOOL.—FULLER SHADE OF MADDER DRAB.

Boil with 2½ lbs. of Barwood.
3½ lbs. of Fustic.
8 ozs. of Logwood.
Sadden with 2 lbs. of Copperas.

———

No. 18.

56 lbs. OF WOOL.—DARK SHADE OF MADDER DRAB.

Boil with 4 lbs. of Barwood.
5 lbs. of Fustic.
2 lbs. of Logwood.
Sadden with 3 lbs. of Copperas.

No. 19.

150 lbs. OF WOOL.—BLUE SLATE COLOR.

Stuff or Boil with 5 lbs. of Logwood.

8 ozs. of Fustic.

Boil one hour and sadden with 12 ozs. of Alum.

———

No. 20.

120 lbs. OF WOOL.—CRANE BLUE.

Stuff with 16 lbs. of Logwood, boil ¾ of an hour.

Sadden with 1½ lb. of Alum, and boil to pattern.

———

No. 21.

90 lbs. OF WOOL.—FANCY BLOOM.

Boil one hour with 8 ozs. of Cudbear.

1¾ lb. of Logwood.

1¼ lb. of Barwood.

Sadden with 1 lb. of Alum.

———

No. 22.

70 lbs. OF WOOL.—SILVER DRAB.

Stuff with 10 ozs. of Logwood.

8 ozs. of Camwood.

Sadden with 3 ozs. of Copperas.

No. 23.

120 lbs. OF WOOL.—REDDER SHADE OF SILVER DRAB.

Stuff with 18 ozs. of Logwood.
10 ozs. of Cudbear.
3 ozs. of Copperas.

No. 24.

60 lbs. OF WOOL.—A VERY LIGHT SHADE OF DRAB.

Dye with 1 oz. of Chemic or good Extract.
4 ozs. of Alum.
10 ozs. of Logwood.
1 oz. of Copperas.
Boil one hour.

No. 25.

120 lbs. OF WOOL.—LIGHT DRAB, YELLOWER SHADE THAN No. 24.

Dye with 6 ozs. of Fustic.
3 ozs. of Logwood.
2 ozs. of Sumach.
$\frac{1}{2}$ oz. of Chemic.
8 ozs. of Alum.
2 ozs. of Copperas.

No. 26.

70 lbs. OF WOOL.—VICUNA DRAB.

Stuff with 5 lbs. of Fustic.
5 lbs. of Mull Madder.
5 lbs. of Crop Madder.
3 lbs. of Camwood.
Sadden with 7 ozs. of Copperas.

———

No. 27.

50 lbs. OF WOOL.—REDDER SHADE OF VICUNA.

Stuff with 5 lbs. of Fustic.
5 lbs. of Mull Madder.
1 lb. of Crop Madder.
2½ lbs. of Camwood.
Sadden with 7 ozs. of Copperas.

These are shades somewhat of the California color.

4

No. 28.

100 lbs. OF WOOL.—FINE RED LÂVENDER.

Stuff with 5 lbs. of Logwood.
3 lbs. of Cudbear.
8 ozs. of Camwood.
Sadden with 10 oz. of Copperas.

When shades are not required so bright, but rather of a flat and dead lavender, add a little Fustic in the stuffing.

No. 29.

120 lbs. OF WOOL.—LIGHT OLIVE.

Stuff with 40 lbs. of Fustic.
3 lbs. of Logwood.
2 lbs. of Camwood.
Sadden with 8 ozs. of Copperas.

No. 30.

120 lbs. OF WOOL.—GREENER OLIVE.

Stuff with 7 lbs. of Fustic.
5 lbs. of Logwood.
5 lbs. of Mull Madder.
6 ozs. of Camwood.
Sadden with 12 ozs. of Copperas.

No. 31.

120 lbs. OF WOOL—REDDER SHADE OF OLIVE.

Stuff with 30 lbs. of Fustic.
20 lbs. of Camwood.
20 lbs. of Mull Madder.
7 lbs. of Crop Madder.
20 ozs. of Logwood.
Sadden with 20 ozs. of Copperas.

No. 32.

135 lbs. OF WOOL.—DARK OLIVE.

Stuff with 60 lbs. of Fustic.
2 ozs. of Alum.
7½ lbs. of Logwood.
10 lbs. of Madder.
Sadden with 1½ lb. of Copperas.
½ lb. of Blue Vitriol.

No. 33.

140 lbs. OF WOOL.—DARKER GREEN OLIVE.

Stuff with 50 lbs. of Fustic.
4 lbs. of Camwood.
9 lbs. of Logwood.
Boil well for an hour and a half.
Sadden with 1 lb. of Alum.
2 lbs. of Copperas.
Boil well in the saddening.

No. 34.

140 lbs. OF WOOL.—DARK GREEN OLIVE, CHROMED.

Prepare or boil an hour with 1½ lb. of Chrome.
12 ozs. of Alum.

Then spread it on the floor all night, and next
  morning

Fill up with 45 lbs. of Fustic.
12 lbs. of Camwood.
6 lbs. of Logwood.

This shade of Olive is similar to that of No.
33, but dyed in quite a different manner. Some
dyers think that the latter mode is the better and
the faster color, but I think it is not so durable
as the former.

The Olive shades are mostly dyed according to
one of these two modes, but neither can be called
fast Olives.

The FAST OLIVE is dyed by being first dyed
Blue in the Woad vat, and then filled up after in
the following manner :—

No. 35.

12 stones OF WOOL.—TRUE OLIVE.

After blueing to about a middle shade in the
  Woad vat,
Stuff with 100 lbs. of Fustic.
20 lbs. of Logwood.
3 lbs. of Madder.
2¼ lbs. of Alum.
Sadden with 2½ lbs. of Copperas.

Darker or lighter shades may be dyed by blueing darker or lighter in the vat, according to shade
required.

Any shade of true Olive may be dyed after this
manner, even down to a Sage Drab, by blueing
light enough in the Woad vat.

———

No. 36.

80 lbs. OF WOOL.—VANT COLOR, NEARLY CANARY COLOR.

Prepare with 1 lb. of Chrome.
8 ozs. of Alum.

Boil an hour, get the wool out, and let it drain
  well, then fill up in a vessel of clean water, with

20 lbs. of Chipped Fustic.
Boil half an hour.
4*

If a redder shade is required, add a little Barwood, as it will cause it to have more of an Orange hue. .

This is not Canary color, which is dyed with Bark or Young Fustic; nor is it so lively, but resembles the light shade of California color.

No. 37.

140 lbs. OF WOOL.—LIGHT BROWN.

Stuff with 60 lbs. of Fustic.
30 lbs. of Camwood.
Boil two hours, then sadden with
2 lbs. of Copperas, and spread.

No. 38.

140 lbs. OF WOOL.—MIDDLE BROWN.

Stuff with 60 lbs. of Fustic.
30 lbs. of Camwood.
1 lb. of Logwood.
Sadden with 1 lb. of Copperas.

No. 39.

100 lbs. OF WOOL.—DARKER BROWN.

Stuff with 45 lbs. of Fustic.
20 lbs. of Camwood.
1½ lb. of Logwood.
Sadden with 1½ lb. of Copperas.

These are good Browns, and will stand Milling, but the Browns dyed first in the Woad vat are more permanent.

—

No. 40.

90 lbs. OF WOOL.—TRUE BROWN.

First blue a light shade in the Woad vat, then stuff with
60 lbs. of Fustic.
10 lbs. of Madder.
2 or 3 lbs. of Camwood.
4 ozs. of Logwood.
Sadden with 1 lb. of Copperas.
4 ozs. of Blue Vitriol.

Either lighter or darker shades of Browns may be dyed after this mode; by dyeing in vat according to shade, darker Blue for darker Browns, and lighter Blues for lighter Browns, or by adding more or less Logwood in the Stuffing, and more or less Copperas in the saddening.

No. 41.

160 lbs. OF WOOL.—LIGHT GREEN.

Dye off with 40 lbs. of Fustic.

2 quarts of Chemic.

4 lbs. of Argol.

8 lbs. of Alum.

Boil one hour.

This is a good bright Green. Darker shades of Green may be dyed by adding more Chemic.

———

No. 42.

70 lbs. OF WOOL.—MOSS GREEN.

This color may be dyed by means of the Chroming process, and filling up with Fustic and Logwood; but as by this mode it is not fast, the proper mode is to blue it in the vat first to shade, and then stuff with

50 lbs. of Fustic.

5 lbs. of Madder.

8 ozs. of Logwood.

2 lbs. of Camwood.

Sadden with 4 ozs. of Copperas.

2 ozs. of Blue Vitriol.

It is difficult to distinguish between the true Green and the other, as such a near resemblance can be produced by the former mode. Nearly all the shades of Green, from this up to the Invisible, and all the various shades of bottle Green may be dyed either with the yellow or blue hue upon them, and will appear equally as good, and can only be distinguished by a test of strong sulphuric acid.

No. 43.

100 lbs. OF WOOL.—A GOOD BOTTLE GREEN, CHROMED.

Boil one hour with 1 lb. of Chrome.

2 lbs. of Alum.

Finish in a vessel of clean water with 30 lbs. of Fustic.

15 lbs. of Logwood.

Boil an hour in the finishing.

No. 44.

100 lbs. OF WOOL.—INVISIBLE GREEN, CHROMED.

Prepare same as No. 43, and finish the same, only add more Logwood and less Fustic. Say,

20 lbs. of Fustic.

30 lbs. of Logwood.

All the various shades of rifles may be dyed after this manner. I will next give a receipt for the true Green.

No. 45.

24 stones OF WOOL.—BOTTLE GREEN, TRUE COLOR.

After dyeing a dark Indigo Blue in the vat, boil
   2 hours with 80 lbs. of Fustic.
40 lbs. of Logwood.
8 ozs. of Alum.

The Invisible is dyed after the same manner,
but still darker; the real fast Green is dyed en-
tirely without Logwood.

———

No. 46.

12 stones OF WOOL.—VIOLET OR MULBERRY.

After being blued to a dark blue in the vat,
Boil one hour with 100 lbs. of Logwood.
10 lbs. of Alum.
5 lbs. of Argol.

Then fish up and add 4 quarts of Nitrate of
Tin; if not dark enough, add more Logwood, and
boil half an hour more. The Plum color, Mul-
berry, and Adelaide have been dyed upon this
mode for the true colors; but the better mode is
that of Chroming first, the same as for Black and
other colors, and then redden and darken with

Cudbear and Logwood, as any shade of darkness may be got by adding more Logwood, and then putting it through the vat. These would be faster colors, and have more solidity about them.

No. 47.

130 lbs. OF WOOL.—FINE CLARET.

Boil two hours with 70 lbs. of Camwood or Sanders.
1 lb. of Logwood.
Sadden with 2½ lbs. of Copperas.

No. 48.

140 lbs. OF WOOL.—DARKER CLARET.

Boil two hours with 70 lbs. of Camwood.
Then take up and let it drain an hour or two, and
Sadden with 3 lbs. of Copperas.
8 lbs. of Logwood.

No. 49.

130 lbs. OF WOOL.—RUSSIAN BROWN.

Stuff with 20 lbs. of Fustic.
40 lbs. of red Sanders.
Sadden with 1 lb. of Copperas.
1 lb. of Alum.

No. 50.

240 lbs. OF WOOL.—DARK BROWN.

Stuff with 130 lbs. of Fustic.

10 lbs. of Crop Madder.

50 lbs. of Camwood.

4 lbs. of Logwood.

Boil two hours, then sadden with 10 lbs. of Copperas.

Smother all night.

No. 51, A.

20 lbs. OF WOOL.—LAC SCARLET.

Dye with 2 lbs. of Brown Tartar.

1 lb. of Young Fustic.

4 lbs. of Lac.

2 quarts of Nitrate of Tin.

Boil one hour.

No. 51, B.

20 lbs. OF WOOL.—FULL PINK.

Dye with 2 lbs. of Tartar.

1 lb. of Alum.

2 lbs. of Cochineal paste.

2 pints of Spirits.

Boil one hour.

No. 52.

20 lbs. OF WOOL.—WINE COLOR.

Dye off with 6 lbs. of Cudbear.

If a Blue shade is wanted, add a little Ammonia, and if a Redder shade, a little Spirits of Salts.

No. 53.

20 lbs. OF WOOL.—ROYAL BLUE.

Dye with 3 lbs. of Prussiate.

3 quarts of Blue Spirits.

The wool must be entered cold, and the liquor heated up to a boil as soon as possible; and when boiled half an hour, take it out and add two pints of Finishing Spirits. If a darker shade is required, add Logwood according to shade with the Finishing Spirits; or it is preferable to add the Logwood at the beginning with the Prussiate for Wools.

Royal Blues that have to stand Milling and Steaming should always have as much Ammonia as Blue Spirits at the beginning, as it makes them much firmer and cleaner.

5

No. 54.

20 lbs. OF WOOL.—GRAIN CRIMSON.

Dye with 2 lbs. of Cochineal paste.
1 lb. of dry Cochineal.
2 pints of Spirits.
2 lbs. of Tartar.

Boil one hour.

No. 55.

20 lbs. OF WOOL.—GRAIN SCARLET.

Dye with 2 lbs. of Tartar.
1½ lb. of Dry Cochineal.
3 pints of Spirits.
2 lbs. of Young Fustic.

Boil one hour.

No. 56.

20 lbs. OF WOOL.—FULL YELLOW.

Dye with 1 lb. of Tartar.
1 lb. of Alum.
4 lbs. of Bark.
2 lbs. of Young Fustic.
2 pints of Spirits.

Boil twenty minutes.

No. 57.

20 lbs. OF WOOL.—ORANGE.

Dye with 8 ozs. of Cochineal.
7 lbs. of Young Fustic.
1 lb. of Tartar.
2 pints of Spirits.

No. 58.

20 lbs. OF WOOL.—CANARY COLOR.

Dye with 1½ lb. of Bark.
1 lb. of Tartar.
1 lb. of Alum.
1 quart of Spirit.

Boil twenty minutes.

No. 59.

20 lbs. OF WOOL.—SKY BLUE.

Dye with ½ a gill of Liquid Extract.
1 lb. of Argol.
2 lbs. of Alum.

Boil twenty minutes.

No. 60.

20 lbs. OF WOOL.—SAXONY BLUE.

Dye with 1 pint of Liquid Extract.
1 lb. of Argol.
2 lbs. of Alum.

Boil twenty minutes.

COTTON-DYEING.

No. 1.

20 lbs. OF COTTON.—BUFF.

After being boiled and properly wet, run through a clear Lime Liquor, then through a weak Copperas Liquor, both cold liquor; repeat in each liquor until the shade be full enough.

Another mode of dying Buff is:—

No. 2.

20 lbs. OF COTTON.—BUFF.

Run the Cotton through Nitrate of Iron, at about 4° Twaddell, and then through a weak Ammonia Liquor in another tub; repeat in each until the shade be full enough.

Both these are firm Buff colors.

5*

No. 3.

20 lbs. OF COTTON.—BUFF, OR NANKIN.

Shave 4 lbs. of Spanish Annotta into 30 gallons of water, to which add 2 lbs. of Pearlash; boil it well up, let it settle, and drain off the clear Liquor; run the Cotton in this Liquor until you get the shade required.

All the various shades of light Buffs, Nankin colors, and Straw colors as well, may be dyed from Annotta by adding little enough of it for the shade. The fine Straw colors which have a yellow tinge have bleached bottoms, that is, they are first bleached, and then dyed in the following manner:—

No. 4.

20 lbs. OF COTTON.—STRAW COLOR.

After being bleached, boil or scald, as may be convenient, 10 lbs. of Fustic in 10 gallons of water, with a few lbs. of Alum, and add clear Liquor according to shade, in a tub of cold water. If fuller shades are wanted, add a little Alum Liquor.

The most lively colors of this class are dyed after this manner for two-colored Damasks, and other goods that are made up with Silk weft.

No. 5.

20 lbs. OF COTTON.—FLESH COLOR.

In a tub of Cold Water, add 2 gallons of spent Annotta, and 1 gallon of Turmeric Liquor; the Turmeric must be boiled up with a little Alum, about 4 ozs. to the gallon of water.

A great variety of shades of this color may be dyed by adding more of the one and less of the other of the two ingredients, Annotta and Turmeric.

No. 6.

20 lbs. OF COTTON.—SAFFLOWER PINK.

Squeeze the Liquor from 4 lbs. of Safflower into a tub; give 10 turns in cold water. If the shade be too blue, add about 1 tot of Oil of Vitriol, and give it a few turns more.

Nearly the same shade may be dyed upon bleached cotton in the following manner :—

First steep it in 4 lbs. of Sumach in a tub, after which it must be spirited in a tub of cold water, with either Muriate or Nitromuriate of Tin. The Liquor must stand at 2° Twaddell. Then add to another tub of cold water 5 lbs. of spent Peachwood. To spend the Peachwood, let it boil a few minutes, or be well scalded, and so with all the other woods.

No. 7.

20 lbs. OF COTTON.—LIGHT PINK.

This shade is dyed in the same manner as No. 6, with the exception of having less Sumach and Peachwood; of Sumach, 2 lbs. instead of 4 lbs., and of Peachwood, 2½ lbs. instead of 5 lbs.

—

No. 8.

20 lbs. OF COTTON.—SCARLET.

It must be first steeped in 4 lbs. of Sumach, then spirited with Muriate of Tin, at 2° Twaddell, and then dyed with 2 lbs. of Peachwood and 3 lbs. of Bark, previously spent; let the Liquor be luke-warm. Give 10 turns, and then wash off for the stove.

If a Yellower shade of Scarlet is required, add more bark: if a Bluer shade, less Bark; if a lighter shade of Scarlet, add less of both Peachwood and Bark; and if a darker shade of Scarlet is required, add more of both Peachwood and Bark.

No. 9.

20 lbs. OF COTTON.—LIGHT CINNAMON BROWN.

Boil up 2 lbs. of Yellow Catechu with 2 gallons of Water, add to it 4 ozs. of Blue Vitriol, and let it boil twenty minutes. In another vessel dissolve 8 ozs. of Chrome, and keep it at the boiling heat; run the Cotton in the Catechu first, give 8 turns, wring out, enter the Chrome tub, give 8 turns more, wring out, and wash off for the stove.

———

No. 10.

20 lbs. OF COTTON.—DARKER SHADE OF LIGHT BROWN.

This shade is dyed the same as No. 9, with the exception of having 2 lbs. of Black Catechu instead of 2 lbs. of Yellow.

When the shade is not Yellow enough, add to the Catechu a little Fustic, or Turmeric, which is preferable. Any shade of Cinnamon Brown may be dyed by varying the Catechu and Turmeric, giving more of the one and less of the other, according to the shade required.

No. 11.

20 lbs. OF COTTON.—DARK SHADES OF BROWN.

These shades must be first steeped in Sumach, then saddened with a little Copperas Liquor in another tub, and a little Urine amongst it, and then dyed in all respects the same as the other two Browns.

No. 12.

20 lbs. OF COTTON.—CHROME YELLOW.

Dissolve 8 ozs. of White Sugar of Lead in one tub, and 8 ozs. of Chrome in another; enter the tub with the Sugar of Lead first, cold, give five turns, and then enter the Chrome, and give five turns, and wring out; enter the other tub again, give five turns more, and then wash off for the stove.

No. 13.

20 lbs. OF COTTON.—DARKER SHADE OF CHROMED YELLOW.

Dissolve 8 ozs. of Brown Sugar of Lead and 8 ozs. of Chrome, each in a separate tub; enter the Sugar of Lead first, give 6 ends, then enter the Chrome, give 6 turns in it; repeat three times in the Sugar of Lead tub, and twice in the Chrome; wash off out of the Sugar of Lead tub for the stove.

No. 14.

20 lbs. OF COTTON.—FULL CHROME ORANGE.

First make up a tub of Cold Water, to which add 4 pailfuls of Lime Lee, or clear Lime Water, enter the Cotton and turn four rounds; dissolve 4 lbs. of Brown Sugar of Lead in 6 quarts of water; in another tub of cold water add 2 quarts of this solution, enter the cotton, give three turns, squeeze out. Enter into another tub of clear lime water, give three turns in this, and in each of the two last tubs, repeat three times, adding to the first tub 1 quart of the solution, and to the other fresh Lime Liquor each time before you enter. Then dissolve 2 lbs. of Chrome in 4 quarts of water, make up a tub at about 20°, and add 2 quarts of the Chrome Liquor; enter the Cotton into this, give three turns, and wring it out; then enter the Sugar of Lead tub, and add 1 quart more of the solution that is left, repeat three times, and add 1 quart of the solution each time, and finish out of the Chrome.

In this state it will appear very uneven, as the

atmosphere affects it very much, but will become even in the raising of it, which is done as follows: Into a pan or vessel of any sort with an open top, add 7 pailfuls of clear Lime Water, bring it just up to the spring and scum it well, do not let it boil, after scumming cool down a little, enter the cotton and give 5 turns. Be careful not to add too much Lime Water, or it will destroy the beauty of the color. This color, like some others, will feel rather rough, and therefore must be run through a little softening, which is made as follows: dissolve 8 ozs. of Pearlash or Soda in 1 gallon of warm Water, to which add 1 pint of Fish Oil, mix it well together, and give it a little of it in a tub of warm water.

No. 15.

20 lbs. OF COTTON.—FAST DRAB.

Boil up 6 lbs. of Mahogany Sawdust.

Draw the clear Liquor into a tub, and give 5 turns.

Raise in the same Liquor with 1 gill of Nitrate of Iron.

The Drabs dyed this way are very fast, and a great variety of Shades may be dyed by adding more or less of the wood according to Shade.

No. 16.

20 lbs. OF COTTON.—FAST BLUE.

To a tub of Cold Water and 1 lb. of Copperas dissolved.

¾ of a Noggin of Muriatic Acid.

Give 5 turns and wring out.

To another Tub of Cold Water add 8 ozs. of dissolved Prussiate.

Give 5 turns and take up.

Add about 1 Noggin of Oil of Vitriol.

Give 5 turns more and wash off for the Stove.

———

No. 17.

20 lbs. OF COTTON.—LAVENDER.

To a tub of Cold Water add 2 lbs. of Logwood previously scalded, and use only the clear Liquor.

Add to it 1 lb. of Alum.

Enter and give 6 or 8 turns.

Lift up and add 8 ozs. of Sweet Extract.

2 lbs. more Alum.

Give 6 turns, and if a Redder Shade is required, add more Logwood Liquor, and if Bluer, more Extract.

6

No. 18.

20 lbs. OF COTTON.—LILAC.

To a tub of Cold Water add 3 lbs. of Logwood.

1½ lb. of Alum, or a little Red Liquor, which is preferable in this class of colors; give 6 or 8 turns. Lighter or darker Shades may be dyed by adding more or less Logwood.

No. 19.

20 lbs. OF COTTON.—SILVER DRAB.

In a tub of Cold Water, add about 4 ozs. of Logwood, and 1 quart of clear Lime Water; give about 8 turns, and wash off for the stove.

No. 20.

20 lbs. OF COTTON.—GOOD LIGHT DRAB.

In a tub of Cold Water add ½ an oz. of Logwood, and 1 lb. of Fustic; give 10 turns, then lift up, and add 8 ozs. of Blue Vitriol, and give 8 turns more, then wash off for the stove.

No. 21.

20 lbs. OF COTTON.—FULLER SHADE OF No. 20.

In all respects dye the same, but add double the quantity of both Fustic and Logwood.

No. 22.

20 lbs. OF COTTON.—LIGHT OLIVE.

In a tub of Cold Water, add 5 lbs. of Fustic, previously scalded, and 1½ lb. of Logwood; give 10 turns, then lift up, and raise by adding 8 ozs. of Blue Vitriol; give 10 turns more, and wash off for the stove.

No. 23.

20 lbs. OF COTTON.—DARKER OLIVE.

In a tub of Cold Water, add 4 lbs. of Sumach; steep in this for an hour. Sadden in another tub of Cold Water, with 2 lbs. of dissolved Copperas, give 8 turns, wring out, enter another tub of warm water with ½ a pailful of Urine. Then dye in another tub with 6 lbs. of Fustic, and raise in the same liquor with 1 lb. of Blue Vitriol.

No. 24.

24 lbs. OF COTTON.—DARK OLIVE.

Dark shades of Olive are dyed same as No. 33, but adding with the Fustic a little Logwood, according to the shade of darkness, and when not Yellow enough, add a little more Fustic Liquor, or Turmeric Liquor, which is preferable for dark colors.

No. 25.

20 lbs. OF COTTON.—FULL YELLOW DRAB.

In a tub of Warm Water, add 8 ozs. of Turmeric, 4 ozs. of Logwood, and 8 lbs. of Fustic; raise in the same Liquor with 2½ lbs. of Alum. Give 10 turns before and 10 turns after saddening, and wash off for the stove.

No. 26.

20 lbs. OF COTTON.—LIGHT BUFF.

In a tub of Cold Water, add a little Nitrate of Iron; give 10 turns, lift up, and raise with a little lime water and a little potash in the same liquor; give a few turns more, and wash off.

No. 27.

20 lbs. OF COTTON.—LIGHT BLUE.

Run through the Copperas Vat one end.

How to dye the same shade with Extract:—

In a tub of Cold Water, add 10 ozs. of Sweet Extract, and 2 lbs. of Alum. Various shades of Light Blue may be dyed with Extract, by adding more or less, according to shade required. Give 10 turns, and then dry off.

———

No. 28.

20 lbs. OF COTTON.—LIGHT EXTRACT GREEN.

In a tub of Water at about 100°, add 8 ozs. of Turmeric, previously scalded; give 10 turns, lift up, and add 4 lbs. of Alum and 1 lb. of Extract, enter again, and give 10 turns more, and then wash off for the stove.

Various shades of Green may be dyed after this manner by adding Extract according to shade. The Extract must be well mixed before it is used.

Greens of this dye are not so permanent as those with a Copperas Vat Blue Bottom.

No. 29.

20 lbs. OF COTTON.—MIDDLE SHADE OF GREEN.

First run the Cotton through the Copperas Vat, and get a moderate shade of Blue, after which wash it well. In another tub add 15 lbs. of scalded Fustic; enter the Cotton, and give 10 turns, lift up, add 4 lbs. of Alum, and give 10 turns more.

If the shade is required bluer, add more Extract in the same Liquor.

No. 30.

20 lbs. OF COTTON.—DARK SHADE OF GREEN.

Dark shades of Green must have a darker Blue bottom, and are dyed in all respects the same as No. 29.

No. 31.

20 lbs. OF COTTON.—CHROMED AND FAST GREENS.

Blue according to the shade required in the Copperas Vat, for light shade of Green. In a tub of Cold Water add 1 lb. of Sugar of Lead, enter the Cotton, and give 5 ends; in another tub of Hot Water add 1 lb. of melted Chrome, give five turns, wring out, repeat twice, and finish off in the Sugar of Lead, and then wash off for the stove.

Dark Chromed Greens are dyed darker in the Copperas Vat first, and have about one-half more Chrome, and are dyed in all respects the same as light Greens.

No. 32.

20 lbs. OF COTTON.—LIGHT CATECHU BROWN.

Spend 3 lbs. of Catechu with 3 ozs. of Blue Vitriol; put this into a tub of Warm Water, enter the cotton, give 8 turns, wring out, and enter another tub of Hot Water with 8 ozs. of Chrome, at the boiling point; give 6 ends, and then wash off for the stove.

No. 33.

20 lbs. OF COTTON.—DARKER CATECHU BROWN.

In a tub of Hot Water, add 4 lbs. of Catechu, give 6 turns; in another tub of Hot Water, add 8 ozs. of Chrome, enter, give five turns, wash out, and repeat once more in each tub, and then wash off for the stove.

No. 34.

20 lbs. OF COTTON.—DARK CATECHU BROWN.

Spend 8 lbs. of Catechu with 8 ozs. of Blue Vitriol, enter the cotton, and for convenience let it stay in it all night, after giving it a few turns. Then in another tub of Hot Water add 1 lb. of Chrome, enter and give a few turns, wash out of the Chrome, and repeat twice or three times.

No. 35.

20 lbs. OF COTTON.—FULL DARK CATECHU BROWN.

A darker class of colors may be dyed by using one-half of Yellow Catechu and one-half of the Black Catechu, and for very Red shades use all Black Catechu.

If very dark shades are required, they must be first Sumached and Saddened, and then dyed in the same way.

No. 36.

20 lbs. OF COTTON.—FULL YELLOW SCARLET.

Scald 4 lbs. of Sumach, and add it to a tub of Cold Water, and steep the cotton in it for a few hours. Make up another tub of Cold Water, and add Nitromuriate of Tin until it stands at 2° Twaddell, enter the cotton into this and give about ten turns. In another tub, add 4 lbs. of Peachwood and 1 lb. of Turmeric, both previously spent, enter the cotton, give 10 turns, and raise in the same Liquor, with 2 lbs. of Alum; let the Liquor be at about 100° Twaddell.

No. 37.

20 lbs. OF COTTON.—BARWOOD RED.

In a tub of Cold Water add 5 lbs. of Sumach, give a few turns and steep in it all night. In another tub of Cold Water add Spirits until it stands at 3° Twaddell, give eight turns, wash in Cold Water, and Warm also. Then in a Copper or Block Tin Vessel add 20 lbs. of Barwood, boil up 15 minutes before the cotton is put in, then cool down a little and enter the cotton, bring it up to a spring boil and turn it on until it comes up to the shade, say about an hour.

No. 38.

20 lbs. OF COTTON.—IMITATION OF TURKEY RED.

This color is dyed the same as Barwood Red, except when it has boiled about an hour, take out of the vessel and add 1 gill of Oil of Vitriol, and boil it a short time longer. The oil will give it a much bluer appearance, and will very much imitate the Turkey Red.

Lighter or darker shades may be dyed by adding more or less of the Barwood.

———

No. 39.

VARIOUS SHADES OF SILVER DRAB.

A good Silver Drab of a very light color may be dyed by first giving a few turns in a little Gall Liquor, and then lift up and add a little Nitrate of Iron, and give a few turns more, and wash off for the stove.

A few Valonias will produce nearly the same effect, but not quite so fine a shade. The Valonias must be boiled with a little water to get the strength out of them.

A great variety of Blue Drabs can be dyed by first Sumaching the cotton, and then in another tub add a little Nitrate of Iron or Copperas liquor, and give a few turns. By adding more Iron or Copperas liquor the shades may be dyed up to dark Slate color, and by adding a little Ammonia, a class of Redder shades may be dyed, and Yellower by adding a little Fustic.

No. 40.

VARIOUS SHADES OF FAWN DRABS.

A great variety of Fawn Drabs may be dyed by adding to a tub of Cold Water a little Catechu, and then a little more according to shades required; and when flatter shades are wanted, add a little Copperas Liquor, which will sadden it. Almost any variety of shade may be dyed after this manner.

Then another class of heavier shades must have a little Sumach with the Catechu, and be saddened with a little Nitrate of Iron, or Copperas Liquor.

No. 41.

20 lbs. OF COTTON.—GOOD BLACK.

In a tub of Cold Water add 5 lbs. of Sumach, give a few turns and steep it all night in the Sumach; then in another tub of cold water add a few pails of Lime Water wring out, in another tub of Cold Water add 2 lbs. of dissolved Copperas, and a pailful of the old Sumach liquor, enter and give 6 turns, then wring out, enter the lime tub again, and give 2 pails more Lime liquor, then scald 6 lbs. of Logwood and 1 lb. of Fustic, add this to another tub of Water, enter the cotton and give 10 turns, lift up, and sadden with a little Copperas in the same liquor.

No. 42.

20 lbs. OF COTTON. — A GOOD BLACK TO STAND MILLING AND SCOURING.

Steep all night with 6 lbs. of Sumach, pass through Lime liquor, and sadden with Copperas as before; repeat in each of the last two tubs, adding more lime and Copperas to each, pass through Logwood and wash off.

Both the last blacks must be softened with a little Oil and Soda Ash.

No. 43.

FAST BLACK.

This Black is first dyed in the Copperas vat, and must have a good Blue bottom, and be dyed in all respects same as No. 42.

No. 44.

20 lbs. OF COTTON.—FAST PURPLE.

This color must have a blue bottom in the Copperas vat, and afterwards it must have a few turns in a tub of Cold Water with a little Muriate of Tin, at 2° Twaddell. In another tub of Water add 4 or 5 lbs. of Logwood, previously spent, enter the cotton and give 8 turns. This is the best purple that can be dyed, possessing a very bright appearance.

Lighter or darker shades may be dyed by adding more or less Logwood according to shade.

No. 45.

20 lbs. OF COTTON.—FAST LAVENDER.

Lavender Shades are dyed the same as No. 44, but are dyed a much lighter blue in the vat, and with less Logwood in the filling up.

These are decidedly the best shades of Lavender that can be dyed, especially for warps which have to be made up with white weft; they will stand any reasonable quantity of Acid, and are much better for the Piece-Dyer.

No. 46.

20 lbs. OF COTTON.—SKY BLUE.

The various shades of light Blues are dyed in the Copperas vat; they can be varied almost to any shade by passing them oftener through.

These shades are much better than the Chinese Blues, which will not stand passing through warm water without washing off.

7

No. 47.

20 lbs. OF COTTON.—BARK YELLOW.

Boil 10 lbs. of Bark in a bag in a vessel of Water for fifteen minutes; take out the bag, and add to the liquor 1 quart of Muriate of Tin, cool down, enter the cotton, and give it 6 turns sharply; if not full enough, take it out and add 1 gill more spirit.

No. 48.

OTHER YELLOWS.

Perhaps the Turmeric Yellow is the cheapest of any, but it is not so permanent as that dyed with Bark or Fustic, and nothing like the Chrome Yellow; though almost any shade of Yellow may be dyed upon cotton, by first boiling in a little Water a very small quantity of Sulphuric Acid, or a little Alum, and using only the clear liquor; 2 or 3 lbs. will dye a fair shade of Yellow upon 20 lbs. of Cotton.

No. 49.

20 lbs. OF COTTON.—PEACHWOOD RED.

Scald 5 lbs. of Sumach, and steep the cotton in it all night. In a tub of Cold Water, add about

1 quart of Spirits, give 10 turns in this, and wash; then scald 5 lbs. of Peachwood, in which liquor work the cotton until you get the shade required.

If a lighter shade is wanted, add less Peachwood.

No. 50.

CRIMSONS AND PINKS.

Various shades of Crimsons and Pinks may be dyed in the following manner :—

First Spirit at about 6° Twaddell, and then enter the Peachwood in quantity according to shade required, whether Crimson or Pink.

This is the quickest way they can be dyed, except by adding both the Spirits and the Wood together, which will answer equally as well. After dyeing a good Crimson, a variety of Pinks may be dyed in the same Liquor, by giving about 6 or 8 turns in it.

No. 51.

20 lbs. OF COTTON.—CLARETS.

For a full Claret, steep the Cotton in 5 lbs. of Sumach all night, then Spirit in another tub at about 2° Twaddell; then wash, scald 3 or 4 lbs. of Logwood, add this to a tub of Warm Water, give 8 turns, lift up, throw out the old Liquor, and add as much more Logwood; give 8 ends more, and raise in the same Liquor, with a little Alum.

Lighter shades are dyed in the same manner, but must have less Wood.

When Redder shades are required, add a little Peachwood and Logwood.

No. 52.

20 lbs. OF COTTON.—RUBY.

Sumach as for Claret, and Spirit the same, then boil up 6 lbs. of Sapanwood in a few gallons of Water; strain off the Liquor, and put it into a tub of Warm Water, give 10 turns and raise with a little Alum.

No. 53.

20 lbs. OF COTTON.—PLUM COLOR.

Prepare with Sumach and Spirits, as before, then boil up 5 lbs. of Logwood and 2 lbs. of Peachwood, or it may be scalded and strained into a tub, to render the liquor clear; give 10 ends, and raise with a little Alum in the same liquor; give 6 ends, and wash off.

No. 54.

20 lbs. OF COTTON.—MAROON.

This color may be dyed in the same manner as No. 52, using Peachwood instead of Sapanwood.

The best mode of dyeing it is by first Sumaching with 5 lbs. of Sumach, and then saddening with 2 lbs. of Copperas, or a little Nitrate of Iron, which is preferable; then wash and enter a tub with 6 lbs. of Peachwood, give 10 turns, lift up, and add 1 pint of Spirits to the same Liquor to raise with; or raise in another tub with Spirits; by adding a little more Spirits, the brightest and fullest Crimson may be dyed, and will stand wearing much better than some other modes of dyeing the same color.

———

No. 55.

20 lbs. OF COTTON.—BLUE PURPLE.

In a tub of Cold Water add 5 lbs. of Sumach, steep in this all night, if convenient; then in another tub spirit with 1 pint of Spirits, and wash out of the spirit tub; then enter another tub with 4 or 5 lbs. of Logwood, give 8 turns, lift up, add 8 ozs. of Tin Crystals, give 8 turns more and wash off.

7*

No. 56.

20 lbs. OF COTTON.—FULL PURPLE.

First Sumach, then sadden with Copperas, wash out of the Copperas, then scald 5 lbs. of Logwood in another tub, and give 10 turns; it will now be a good black, but must be raised with a pint of Spirits in the same tub.

Purple warps dyed on this principle are very good and permanent.

No. 57.

20 lbs. OF COTTON.—SAXON BLUE.

This color may be dyed in the Copperas vat, but not so bright as with Prussiate of Potash. To dye with Prussiate it must be first ironed or turned in a tub of Cold Water with about 1 quart of Nitrate of Iron until it becomes a light buff; it must then pass through weak Ammonia in another tub, then wash it; dissolve about 1 lb. of Prussiate and add it to another tub of Cold Water, give about ten turns, then lift up, and add 1 noggin of Oil of Vitriol, enter again, and give 10 turns, and wash off for the Stove.

For darker shades add more Prussiate.

No. 58.

20 lbs. OF COTTON.—FLAT ROYAL BLUE.

This color is first dyed in the Copperas vat, and then dyed in the same way as No. 57, so that by having a vat blue bottom it takes less Prussiate.

———

No. 59.

20 lbs. OF COTTON. — BRIGHT ROYAL BLUE.

In the first tub make up a decoction of Nitrate of Iron, at 3° Twaddell, about 3 pints, give 6 turns; in another tub of Water add 3 lbs. of dissolved Prussiate, give 6 turns, lift up, and add 1 gill of Oil of Vitriol, give 6 turns more. To the tub with the Iron in, add 1 lb. of Tin Crystals, pass through the Iron 4 times, and through the Prussiate 3 times.

———

No. 60.

VICTORIA BLUE.

This color is dyed in most respects same as No. 59, but with this difference, the Crystals of Tin are added to the Iron at the beginning, and the Oil of Vitriol is not added until the last time in the Prussiate. There is little difference in these two blues; the latter may be somewhat more bloomy.

———

No. 61.

20 lbs. OF COTTON.—NAPOLEON BLUE.

This is the most bloomy shade that has yet been produced upon Cotton Fabrics or Cotton Yarns. In the first place add 1 quart of Muriate of Tin to a tub of cold water, enter the cotton and give 8 turns; in another tub add the clear liquor from 4 lbs. of Logwood, then add to another tub of cold water 2 quarts of Nitrate of Iron, and 2 lbs. of Crystals of Tin, enter the cotton and give 6 turns, then in another tub add 3 lbs. of melted Prussiate, enter this and give 6 turns, repeat 2 or 3 times; then to the Prussiate add 1 gill of Oil of Vitriol, pass through, and wash off for the Stove.

———

No. 62.

ON BLEACHING COTTON.

The Warps or Yarns are first steeped in Pearlash Liquor, at boiling point, to soften the grease and dirt. Some Bleachers wash out in warm Pearlash Liquor, after which they are passed through a solution of Chloride of Lime; then they are washed in more Pearlash water. Both these processes are repeated until the goods become sufficiently White; they are then taken and boiled in a weak solution of Pearlash and White Soap, which removes all smell of the Chlorine, and gives to the Cotton a beautiful whiteness.

A much readier way of Bleaching is that of steeping the cotton as in the former mode, and then passing it through Chloride of Lime and Oil of Vitriol until it assumes a good white appearance. Care must be taken not to use too much Oil of Vitriol, as that would have a tendency to destroy the strength of the fabric.

No. 63.

HOW TO SPEND CATECHU.

Let it be well boiled with 1 or 2 ozs. of Blue Vitriol to every pound of Catechu, and about 10 times its weight of water.

No. 64.

HOW TO MAKE THE SPIRITS FOR COTTON-DYEING PURPOSES.

Add 1 lb. of Aqua Fortis to 5 lbs. of Spirits of Salts, and kill them with about $2\frac{1}{2}$ ozs. of Tin to the pound. The Tin may be all added at first either in a bottle or in a jar.

No. 65.

ON STEEPING.

Warps and Hanks should be well wet before they are dyed, or they will not dye even; they should be steeped in boiling water for a few hours at least, or boiled, if convenient, so as to penetrate through every thread.

No. 66.

HOW TO SPEND ANNOTTA.

It must be well boiled with about 1 gallon of water to the pound, and ¾ lb. of Pearlashes.

No. 67.

HOW TO SPEND TURMERIC FOR COTTON-DYEING.

It must be boiled up with water, and much of the strength will bleed out of it without acid or alkali; but about 8 ozs. of Alum to 1 lb. of Turmeric is generally used. Pearlash will bleed more strength out of it, but it will not dye so bright and clear a Yellow, but it will be more of the Olive cast.

No. 68.

HOW TO SPEND SAFFLOWER.

In the first place put the quantity required into a bag, and steep it in water for a few hours to soften it, then it must be trodden well and rinsed again in the Water, and so on repeatedly until all the Yellow coloring matter is extracted, as it is of no use whatever to dyers; then the flowers will have a bright crimson appearance, and must be put to steep in cold water sufficient to cover them, and to every pound of Flower there must be added 8 ozs. of Pearlash, previously dissolved, and afterwards well mixed amongst the flowers so as to extract all the Red coloring matter from them; it will take a few hours to do this; it must then be squeezed either between the hands or in a press, and the clear liquor used for dyeing purposes. Alone it will dye a very Blue shade of Pink, but requires a little Tartaric or Sulphuric Acid to redden it, when a Red shade is required.

It should be well rubbed before it is put into the bags to steep in the water.

SILK-DYEING.

No. 1.

10 lbs. OF SILK.—LAVENDER.

In a tub of warm water, at 20°, add 1 lb. of Extract of Indigo, 4 lbs. of Alum, previously dissolved, and a little Plum Liquor, according to the shade of redness required.

By adding more Extract, a darker shade may be dyed, and a lighter by adding less of it.

By varying the quantities of Extract and Plum Liquor, all the various shades of Lavender may be dyed.

No. 2.

10 lbs. OF SILK.—LAVENDER, No. 2.

Another mode of dyeing the foregoing colors is as follows: First dye the Silk, at boiling heat, with a little Cudbear, according to the shade of redness required, and afterwards make up a tub of warm water, at about 20°, and add 4 lbs. of

Alum, and Extract according to the shade of blueness it requires.

———

No. 3.

10 lbs. OF SILK.—LAVENDER.

Make up a tub of warm water, at about 20°, add 1 lb. of Extract, and in the place of Alum add Red Liquor, and Logwood, about 2 or 3 quarts.

The Logwood must be boiled up with the Red Liquor, about 2 lbs. of Logwood to a gallon. Any variety of shades may be dyed in this way.

Another mode of dyeing the Red shades of Lavender is by passing them through the Plum vat when it is nearly worn out for the Plum colors.

———

No. 4.

SPIRIT YELLOWS.

This color is dyed by being passed through strong Nitric Acid, and then through a little Soda or Soda ashes in warm water.

This will produce a good full Yellow or light Orange.

No. 5.

WOLD YELLOW.

In a Copper boil up a bunch of Wold, say 4 lbs., fasten it in the bottom of the vessel, add a few ounces of Pearlash, then put into another vessel as much of this clear Liquor as the shade may require, with about 4 ozs. of Alum.

The Wold Yellows are very light bright colors, and very fast.

———

No. 6.

10 lbs. OF SILK.—BARK YELLOW.

Boil up in a bag about 4 lbs. of Quercitron Bark either in a Copper or clean Tub, add 2 lbs. of Alum and 1 pint of Nitrate or Muriate of Tin.

This will produce a good full shade of Yellow, and, by adding more or less of Bark and Spirits, any shade of Yellow may be dyed.

———

No. 7.

10 lbs. OF SILK.—TURMERIC YELLOW.

In a tub scald about 4 lbs. of Turmeric, and dye with the clear Liquor; in another tub, at boiling heat, add 1 gill of Oil of Vitriol, and use Liquor according to shade.

Any shade of Yellow, from the lightest to the darkest, may be dyed from Turmeric, though it is very fugitive.

Some dyers pass it through a little Soda afterwards. It has a tendency to soften the silk and raise the color.

No. 8.

ORANGE COLOR.

In a tub of boiling Soap Lather, add Annotta, according to shade, and turn the Silk on sharply; when up to the pattern pass through cold water so that you may wring out; wash twice through cold water, and wring up.

The Annotta Liquor for this color must be very strong. To make the Liquor, add 2 lbs. of Annotta to 1 gallon of boiling Ash Liquor, to be well boiled, so that every particle may be dissolved, and only use the clear Liquor. All the various shades of Orange color may be dyed by adding more or less Annotta.

No. 9.

10 lbs. OF SILK.—GRAIN CRIMSON.

In a tub of warm water, at 110°, add 3 pints of Nitrate of Tin (or Aqua Fortis killed with Tin), turn the Silk in this Liquor from two to three hours, then wring it out, and stick it up again for the Cochineal. Scald 3¼ lbs. of Cochineal with boiling water, that is, about 3½ ozs. of Cochineal to each pound of Silk, put it into a bag, and fill a tub with boiling water, and let it be poured through the bag into the tub, so as to get all the strength out of the Cochineal. Then enter the Silk, give a few turns, and steep in the Liquor all night. In the morning, wring it out, and part the skeins for blueing, if not blue enough. Get a tub of clean cold water, and put a few gallons of the Cochineal Liquor into it, which will prevent the Silk from having a black appearance, to which it is subject, and blue in it; the more cold water it has, the bluer it will appear.

This mode of dyeing Crimsons is the best that can be produced, and if there were no other Receipt in this book, this is worth the price of it.

———

No. 10.

10 lbs. OF SILK.—GRAIN SCARLET.

Stuff or dye in a Soap Lather with Annotta, boiling hot, until you have a good full Orange bottom, about the same as No. 8. Wash well out of the Annotta, and then dye same as Crimson, see No. 9, only add less Cochineal; if a moderate shade is required, about 2¾ ozs. to the pound, but if a full shade is wanted, 3½ ozs. to the pound.

No. 11.
SKY BLUES FROM EXTRACT.

In the first place dissolve the quantity of Extract required in warm water, and then put in a quantity of wool, which will take up or absorb the Extract; afterwards put the wool into another vessel, and add a little Pearlashes to discharge the Extract from the wool again, and put the Silk in the same Liquor. By this means the color will be much brighter than if the Extract was put upon the Silk without being put upon the wool. It must then be washed off in a little warm water with a little Oil of Vitriol. If the color is not sufficiently bloomy, pass it through a little liquid Archil in warm water. This will put a bright bloomy appearance upon it. When the color is not required to be very bright, the Extract may be put upon the Silk with a little Alum, at about 100°.

No. 12.
SKY BLUES FROM PRUSSIATE.

In a tub of cold water add Nitrate of Iron until it stands at about 1° Twaddell, give the silk a few turns, then pass it through weak Ammonia Liquor, say about a pint to 30 gallons. In another tub add Prussiate Liquor according to shade required; one ounce to the pound will make a fine Light

8*

Blue : if a darker shade is required, more Prussiate must be added.   After giving a few turns, lift up and add about a noggin of Oil of Vitriol, put down again and give a few more turns, and wash off.

———

No. 13, A.

10 lbs. OF BLUE.—MAZARINE BLUE.

In a copper or tub at boil, add 6 lbs. of Liquid Archil, give a few turns and then pass through the Indigo vat.   Either the Copperas or Woad vat will answer, but the Woad vat is preferable.

———

No. 13, B.

10 lbs. OF SILK.—FRENCH BLUE.

Give 6 turns in a tub of cold water with Nitrate of Iron at 6° Twaddell, then steep the silk in the same liquor for about 40 minutes, wring out and wash well, then give 12 turns in common Soda water, say 1 lb. of it in 24 gallons of water at 120°, wring out, and without washing enter the Prussiate, 1½ lb. in 30 gallons of water, to which add 1 quart of Spirits of Salts (Muriatic Acid), and give 10 turns, then lift up and add 1 quart more Salts, give 10 turns more, and wash out. In this state the silk will appear a very dull color ; it must then be passed through weak Ammonia Liquor. To 30 gallons of water at 20° add 1 gill of Ammonia, give 6 turns, then dry it sharply.

By passing it through this it will be raised to a very dark bloomy Blue, something like the Mazarine.

No. 14.

10 lbs. OF SILK.—ROYAL BLUE.

Make up a tub of Nitrate of Iron at 6°, to which add 1 pint of good Muriate of Tin and 4 ozs. of Tartaric Acid, turn it in this for about 1 hour. In another tub add 1½ lb. of dissolved Prussiate and 1 gill of Oil of Vitriol, wash out of the Iron tub and enter the Prussiate tub, repeat in the Iron twice and once in Prussiate, wash out of the Iron. In another tub add a little Oil of Vitriol until it tastes sour, give 6 turns in this to clear off any rust that may adhere to it. More Prussiate will produce a darker color, and less a lighter, but the same quantity of Iron and Tin must be used.

No. 15.

10 lbs. OF SILK.—BLUE BLACK.

Steep in Nitrate of Iron, at 4° for about 1 hour, wring out and wash it. Make up a tub at about 120°, add the clear Liquor from Logwood previously scalded, about the same weight as the silk, and a pailful of melted Soap to keep up a lather, give 12 turns; if not dark enough, add a little more Logwood.

———

No. 16.

10 lbs. OF SILK.—COMMON FULL BLACK.

Steep in Nitrate of Iron at 4° for about 1 hour, after giving the Silk a few turns, wring out and wash well in a tub of warm water at about 120°, add 15 lbs. of Logwood, scalded, and add only the clear liquor, and 5 lbs. of scalded Fustic, and a little melted Soap. If the color is not flat enough, add a little more Fustic liquor, and if not dark enough, add more Logwood.

———

No. 17.

BROWNS OF DIFFERENT SHADES.

For a good light Brown, stuff with Annotta liquor in a Soap lather up to a good orange in boiling water, after this wash well and sadden in a weak Copperas liquor cold, let the Copperas liquor be very clear, then wash off and dye with Fustic and Archil. All the light shades of Browns may be dyed after this manner. When a rather darker shade is required, sadden rather stronger.

The yellowness of the color must be regulated with the Fustic, and the redness with the Archil, according to the shade required.

No. 18.

DARK BROWNS OF DIFFERENT SHADES.

Stuff with Annotta in boiling water until you obtain a full Orange. Sadden with stronger Copperas Liquor, and then dye with Fustic, Archil, and Logwood.

Any shade required in Browns may be dyed after this manner, but it is impossible to point out every tinge and hue, as in Browns they are so varied. The Fustic produces the Yellow part of the color, the Archil the red part, and the Logwood the darkness or the Blue part, after the Copperas or saddening.

No. 19.

CALIFORNIA BROWNS AND OLIVE.

Another mode of dyeing Browns.

Put on a strong Annotta bottom, as in the other Browns, at boiling point, and wash well out of it; then scald Fustic, and add the clear Liquor according to shade, and a little Sumach Liquor along

with it. Then sadden in cold water with a little
Argol and Copperas Liquor, and when the shade
is wanted of a very Olive cast, add a little Turme-
fic with the Fustic.

All the bright colors in Snuff Brown, California colors, and light Olive are dyed according to
this Receipt. The darkness of the color must be
regulated by the Sumach and Copperas.

————

No. 20.

RED OR CLARET BROWN.

This class of colors is dyed with Annotta bottoms, as before, and then passed through the Plum
vat. They are perhaps the richest Browns that
can be produced, and are dyed better by this
means than by any other. But for the information of those who are desirous of understanding
the different modes of dyeing the same color by
different ingredients, and in different modes, I
will next insert another mode of dyeing the Red
Browns.

————

No. 21.

ANOTHER MODE OF DYEING RED BROWNS.

First steep the Silk in Alum, at about 6° Twaddell, for about 1 hour, then wash it well in Cold

Water; scald Logwood, Peachwood, and Fustic separately, and use the clear Liquor. The Logwood must be used very sparingly, as it will darken very fast. The Peachwood must be the strongest, and Fustic in a moderate way, as

6 parts of Peachwood,
4 parts of Fustic,
1 part of Logwood.

Using quantity according to shade required, at about 140°. From the lightest to the darkest shades may be dyed after this manner. These Browns are dyed sooner and cheaper than the saddened Browns, but are not so permanent.

No. 22.

SOUR BROWNS.

Almost any shade of Brown may be dyed in the following manner, and by varying the ingredients according to shade required: Dye with Camwood, Chemic, and Acid.

No. 23.

LIGHT CLARET BROWNS.

Dye with 2 lbs. of Camwood, to each pound of Silk add Oil of Vitriol and a little Red Argol for the sour; boil 1 hour in a clean copper, and then sadden with a little Chemic.

No. 24.

DARK CLARET BROWNS.

Stuff with 3 lbs. of Camwood to each lb. of Silk, add a little Argol and Oil of Vitriol for the acid, boil an hour and a half, and wash it well out of this liquor, and sadden in cold water with Copperas liquor. The Camwood must be boiled in bags.

No. 25.

CLARETS AND CHOCOLATES.

Steep in Alum, at 6° Twaddell, for about one hour, wash well out, and then dye with Peachwood and Logwood, according to shade; if a Claret, use very little Logwood, and if a Chocolate, use a little more, but most Peachwood, in all cases. Dye at about 160°.

All the various shades of Claret and Chocolate may be dyed by adding more or less of the two ingredients, Peachwood and Logwood.

No. 26.

ANOTHER MODE OF DYEING CLARETS AND CHOCOLATES.

Boil with Alum and Peachwood together, and then finish in another vessel with Logwood, according to the darkness required.

The body of color in this mode of dyeing is put on in the boiling, and the Logwood is used to blue and darken the same.

No. 27.

MOCK CRIMSONS, DYED DIFFERENT WAYS.

These colors are dyed by first boiling in Alum, and are then finished with Peachwood Liquor and a little Muriate of Tin, at boiling point.

Another mode is by steeping the Silk in Alum for a few hours, and then dyeing at the boiling point, with Peachwood only.

But the best and readiest mode is by dyeing it off at once with Peachwood Liquor and Muriate of Tin, as either light or dark shades may be dyed by adding Peachwood according to shade required.

These are all different from the Crimson Vat colors.

No. 28.

OLIVE.

In the first place, sadden the Silk with Copperas Liquor, wash out, and dye with Fustic, moderately strong, at boiling heat. Darken with Logwood, blue with Chemic, and when to pattern,

9

wash off in cold water, with a little Oil of Vitriol to preserve the Chemic.

Lighter and darker shades may be dyed by varying the quantity of Logwood.

No. 29.

PURPLES.

A variety of Purples may be dyed by first steeping the Silk in Alum, and afterwards dyeing with Logwood and Oxalic Acid.

No. 30.

MAROONS.

Various shades of Maroons may be dyed with Lima Peachwood, Muriate of Tin, and Alum, at boiling point.

No. 31.

MAROONS, ANOTHER WAY.

Dye with Cudbear, at boiling heat, and add a little Young Fustic and Muriate of Tin.

Any shade of Maroon may be dyed by adding or diminishing the Cudbear, according to shade required.

No. 32.

RUBY.

The Ruby is dyed from Cudbear alone; it will produce a fine color of itself. When a Blue shade is required, add a little Ammonia, and when a Red shade is required, add a little Muriate of Tin.

No. 33.

DAUNCE BLACK.

Give 10 turns in Nitrate of Iron at 4°, then fill up with Prussiate, about 2 ozs. to the pound, repeat twice, wash out of the Iron, and sadden with Copperas.

If a darker shade is required, pass through a little Logwood.

This color is dyed with a Blue bottom, so that it may not be discharged or spotted with Acid, as Blacks are generally subject to be.

No. 34.

VIOLET.

A variety of shades of this color may be dyed by first steeping the Silk in Alum, and then dyeing with a little Cudbear and Logwood, according to shade.

If a very blue shade is required, add a little Ammonia, and if a red shade is required, add a little Alum with the Cudbear. Clean cold water will blue this class of colors. The Violets are not all dyed in this manner: some are dyed in a Plum Vat.

No. 36.

10 lbs. OF SILK.—LIGHT GREEN.

In a tub of cold water, add 6 lbs. of dissolved Alum, give the Silk a few turns, steep it in the same Liquor all night and wash it out next morning. Boil up 10 lbs. of chipped Ebony Wood, put the clear Liquor into another tub of water, at 100°, give 6 turns, lift up, and add about 1 gill of Extract of Indigo, or more, according to shade required.

No. 37.

10 lbs. OF SILK.—MIDDLE GREEN.

Steep in Alum for about twelve hours, same as No. 36, wash out of the Alum, boil up 20 lbs. of Fustic, and use the clear liquor, at about 120°; give 10 turns, then lift up, and add Extract according to shade required.

If a yellower shade is required, add more Fustic, or a little Turmeric Liquor.

No. 38.

10 lbs. OF SILK.—DARK GREEN.

Steep the Silk same as in last Receipt, and dye in a tub of water, at about 120°, with Fustic or Turmeric Liquor, and Extract, according to shade.

No. 39.

BOTTLE GREEN.

The Bottle Green and Dark Olive shades are dyed in all respects the same as the foregoing Greens, but must be passed through Copperas Liquor, and then in another tub of lukewarm water add a little Logwood Liquor.

No. 40.

OTHER GREENS OF DIFFERENT SHADES.

In a tub of water, at 140°, add about 4 lbs. of Alum, and Fustic Liquor, Extract, and Chemic, according to shade. Dye off in this, and when according to pattern, wash in cold water, to which add a little Oil of Vitriol to keep the Blue on the Silk.

By this mode of dyeing Greens, all the various

9*

shades may be got, and any tinge or hue, by adding Fustic or Turmeric Liquor, according to tint required. It is a readier mode of dyeing the Greens, and equally as good.

No. 41.

FAST GREEN WITH A BLUE BOTTOM.

First pass the silk through the Copperas vat, and put on the body of blue required for the shade, then dye at boiling heat with Fustic according to shade required, with a little Alum for the sour to work on the Fustic. When an Olive shade is required, add a little Turmeric. All shades of middle and dark Green may be dyed after this receipt, and the colors dyed in this way are not so soon stained as the other; they are also more durable by having a vat bottom.

No. 42.

LIGHT OLIVES, OF DIFFERENT SHADES.

This class of colors is the best with a light Blue bottom, and dyed off at the boiling point, with Turmeric Liquor and a little Archil.

When the Green shade is required, add a little Turmeric only, and when a Redder shade is required, add a little Archil also. Some of the finest colors may be produced after this manner. The bright Acanthuses, Ottoman Leaves, and Bronzes are dyed in this way.

———

No. 43.

10 lbs. OF SILK.—FLESH COLOR OR BUFF.

Make up a tub, at boiling point, with a little White Soap, 4 ozs. of Pearlash, and 2 quarts of Annotta Liquor; enter the Silk, and turn on until it be dyed to pattern.

Lighter or darker shades may be dyed by adding more or less Annotta Liquor.

———

No. 44.

10 lbs. OF SILK.—SALMON.

This color is dyed the same as Flesh color, but must be passed through a little Muriate of Tin in a tub of warm water afterwards, in order to raise the Redness of the color.

———

No. 45.

10 lbs. OF SILK.—GOLD COLOR.

Dye at boiling heat in a Soap lather, with Annotta according to shade required. If a full shade is required, a full shade of Annotta color must be put upon the Silk, and if lighter shades are required, a lighter bottom must be put on. After which, boil up 4 lbs. of Bark, with 1 quart of Muriate of Tin; the Bark must be put into a bag. Cool the vessel down a little, enter the Silk, and turn it for about twenty minutes.

If it is not yellow enough, take out the Silk, and put it in the bag with 1 pint more of Tin Spirits, boil it a little, and then enter the Silk again.

———

No. 46.

10 lbs. OF SILK.—YELLOW FAWN DRAB.

To a tub of warm water add 1 quart of Annotta Liquor, 1 lb. to a gallon of water, and 8 ozs. of Pearlash; to this add 2 lbs. of scalded Fustic and 8 ozs. of Sumach; enter, give 10 turns, lift up, and throw out a few pailfuls of the Liquor; dissolve 8 ozs. of Argol and 2 lbs. of Copperas in 1 gallon of water, add 1 quart of this to the Liquor, and if not flat enough add more of it.

No. 47.

10 lbs. OF SILK.—FAWN DRAB.

To a tub of warm water, add 1 pint of Annotta Liquor, 1 lb. of Sumach, and 1 lb. of Fustic; and sadden down with Copperas Liquor, according to shade.

———

No. 48.

10 lbs. OF SILK.—FLAT DRAB.

To a tub of warm water add 1 gill of Annotta, 1 lb. of Fustic, 1½ lb. of Sumach, and sadden in another tub of cold water with Copperas Liquor, according to the shade of deadness required.

———

No. 49.

HEAVY DRABS.

Dye in a killed Liquor, at about 100°, with a little Fustic Liquor, a little Archil, and a little Chemic.

Any shade of Drabs of a heavy, flat, or dark appearance may be dyed in this way, from these ingredients.

The Liquor is said to be killed, when a quantity of Copperas Liquor is poured into it. For these shades it requires about ½ a noggin to 10 lbs. of Silk.

No. 50.

SLATE DRAB.

Dye in killed Liquor with a little Fustic Liquor, and a little Logwood Liquor; if not Blue enough, add a little Chemic.

No. 51.

10 lbs. OF SILK.—BRONZE DRAB.

In a tub of warm water, at 100°, add 1 lb. of Fustic and 6 ozs. of Archil, and then sadden with Copperas Liquor.

These shades of Drab are all very distinct, the last three especially. Perhaps there is as much difference in the shades as is possible to be made in Drabs; but all the varieties of shades that come between these may be dyed according to the preceding Receipts, which is the way that most drabs are dyed. I will now give a few Receipts of another mode of dyeing Fawns by means of Acid instead of a killed Liquor.

Almost all Silk requires to be passed through a mode of softening, as it is called by Silk-Dyers. It is made as follows: Add 2 lbs. of Sweet Oil to 1 lb. of Sulphuric Acid (Oil of Vitriol), and stir it quickly when mixing. This will form a sort of paste, which will mix with water, not floating on the top, like Oil. A little of this must be added to a tub of cold water, and the Silk passed through it, which will give it a very smooth finish, and cause it to spin much better than it otherwise would.

No. 52.

ANOTHER MODE OF DYEING DRABS.

A great variety of Drabs may be dyed, at boiling heat, with a little Oil of Vitriol for the sour, and a little Argol. Many of the Fawn shades would require only a little liquid Archil and Madder Liquor, less or more, according to shade.

Some of the brightest colors of light Fawns may be dyed in this manner; and by adding a little Chemic to flatten or sadden with, a still greater variety may be dyed. The colors dyed in this manner are firmer and less liable to stain than those dyed in a killed Liquor.

No. 53.

SOUR BROWNS.

A great variety of Browns may be dyed with Acid, using Camwood for the Red part of the color, Turmeric for the Yellow part, and then sadden with Copperas in another vessel cold. After a good body of Camwood is got upon the Silk, it may be saddened down to either a light or a dark shade.

———

No. 54.

FRENCH WHITE.

This color is first bleached, and then dyed with Archil and Chemic. Make up a tub at about 160°, to which add a little liquid Archil, and either a little Chemic or Extract, with a pailful of Soap Lather. This will put down the Yellowness of color, and raise it to a fine clear White. Be careful not to add too much of either Archil or Chemic, as it requires very little.

Another mode of dyeing a White is by stoving it with Sulphur.

———

No. 55.

PINKS FROM SAFFLOWER.

The Safflower for Light Pinks is first put upon cotton, and then discharged from the cotton, and then put upon the silk in the following manner: The Safflower is spent with Pearlashes in the usual way, and the Liquor put into a vessel with water, and then a quantity of either Cotton Yarns or Cotton Wool steeped in the Liquor, so as to take up the strength of it.

The Cotton must then be put into another vessel of clean water, with a portion of Pearlashes, which will discharge the strength of the Safflower from the cotton, and clear it from all dirt. The silk must then be dyed in the same Liquor with a little Oil of Vitriol. The whole of this process must be cold. By this means the color will be clear and bright.

No. 56.

PINKS FROM PEACHWOOD.

This color may be dyed either by being passed through the Crimson Vat, or by first steeping the Silk in Alum, and then dyeing it with Peachwood, at boiling heat; by using a little Muriate of Tin the color will be much brighter.

No. 57.

GRAIN PINKS.

This class of Pinks may be dyed in various ways. One manner is: first pass the Silk through Red Liquor, and then dye, at boiling heat, with the clear Liquor from scalded Cochineal.

10

Another mode is: first steep it in Alum, and dye same as when passed through Red Liquor.

And another mode is by dyeing it the same as dyeing Grain Crimson, only using much less Cochineal.

———

No. 58.

MOCK SCARLET.

Get a good Annotta bottom on, the same as for the other Scarlet, until it appears a good Orange; then wash, and spend about 4 or 5 lbs. of Peachwood to 10 lbs. of Silk; add the clear Liquor to a tub of hot water, give 10 turns, and then pass through the Crimson Vat.

Another mode is to dye it, at boiling heat, with Peachwood Liquor and Muriate of Tin; after the Annotta, Orange is put on it as in the other mode.

———

No. 59.

REAL PARIS BLACKS.

In a tub of water, at 180°, made up with 3 parts of Fustic, and 1 part of Bark Liquor, add 2 ozs. of Verdigris, and 1 oz. of Copperas to every pound of Silk. Steep the Silk in this all night, after giving it a few turns. In the morning, wring out, and wash well twice over. Then make the Silk up for dyeing in a Logwood Liquor, at 150°. This must be dyed in a Soap Lather. If the shade required be a dark one, much Logwood must be used; if it has a green appearance, use more Logwood, and when dark enough wash twice over. Then stick up the Silk for softening in warm water. The softening must be a little Soda and Neat's-foot Oil. This is the best Black that can be dyed.

———

No. 60.

NAPOLEON BLUE, AND HOW TO MAKE THE SPIRITS FOR THE SAME.

Into a tub put 100 lbs. of Spirits of Salts (Muriatic Acid), to which add 7 lbs. of Feathered Tin; put the jar into boiling water, and keep up the heat until the tin be all eaten away. Into another jar about the same size put the same quantity of Spirits of Salts, to which add Iron filings until it will eat no more (it will be continually eating for two or three days, and will require to be kept warm all the time), and after settling it will be ready for use. This is the real Muriate of Iron, the former the real Muriate of Tin.

Some prefer Nitrate of Iron to Muriate of Iron, which may be made as follows:—

Into a jar of about the same size put about the same quantity of Aqua fortis (Nitric Acid), at about 20° Twaddell, to which add Iron filings, as in the other Spirits, until it will eat no more; add only a little of it at once, as it is subject to boil over when too much is added at a time; it will not require heat as the other Spirit.

These are the Spirits to be used in proportion as follows: Into a half-pipe tub of cold water add 2 quarts of the Muriate of Tin, and the same quantity of Muriate or Nitrate of Iron, and 1 lb. of Tartaric Acid. This is the Mordant for the Silk.

In another tub of the same size add 6 lbs. of Alum, previously dissolved. Then add 2 ozs. of the Red Prussiate of Potash to every lb. of Silk to be dyed. In this, give the Silk 10 turns; the Liquor must be at about 100°; then slightly wash, enter the Mordant tub, give 10 turns, wring out, wash it again, and repeat in each until you get the shade required. It may require 5 or 6 rounds, or more, according to the darkness of the color. This will dye a good color; if a Bluer shade is required, add more of the Nitrate or Muriate of Iron, and less of Muriate of Tin; and if a Redder shade is required, add more of the Muriate of Tin, and less of the Nitrate or Muriate of Iron for the Mordant.

The Yellow Prussiate of Potash will produce nearly the same shade of color, with the same weight of it as of the Red.

The Silk must pass through the Mordant the last, and not through the Prussiate; after which, it must be washed out and put to soak in Fuller's earth for a few hours; then wash it out of the earth, and pass it through the Mordant again with about 10 turns more; then wring it out, not wash it, ready for getting up. In another tub of cold water add a little Tartaric Acid, sufficient to keep the color; to a spoonful of the best Oil add the least drop of Oil of vitriol, put this into the tub, and give the Silk a few turns, and then wring it out. If the Silk does not appear dark enough, dry it hot; but if dark enough, dry it cool.

This is for the first day's work; the second will not require so many dye-wares. For the next day's work, only add about one-half of the Spirits of each kind, and for the Mordant, much of the strength of the other will be left in the tub. Take the clear liquor from the Prussiate tub and throw down the sediment, and add only $1\frac{1}{2}$ oz. of Prussiate to the pound of Silk in the place of 2 ozs.; heat up to 100°, and add about the same quantity of Alum as before, and dye in all respects the same as the previous day.

10*

WOOLLEN YARN DYEING.

No. 1.

20 BUNCHES 44s.—PEA GREEN, VERY FINE SHADE.

Dye at boiling heat with 2 lbs. of Alum,
10 lbs. of Wold,
8 ozs. of Liquid Extract,
1 lb. of Brown Tartar, and
1 gill of Spirits.

Flatter Greens about the same shades may be dyed without Spirit and Wolds, by using Fustic in the place of both; but the color will not be anything like the same in point of brightness.

No. 2.

6 GROSS OF 30s.—SILVER DRAB.

Dye with 4 ozs. of Logwood,
1 oz. of Cudbear, and
4 ozs. of Alum.

No. 3.

16 BUNCHES 36s.—CALIFORNIA COLOR.

Dye with 5 lbs. of Crop Madder.
2 lbs. of Camwood.
2 lbs. of Fustic.
2 ozs. of Alum.
1 lb. of Copperas.

No. 4.

24 BUNCHES.—BRIGHT VICUNA.

Dye with 5 lbs. of Crop Madder.
2 lbs. of Fustic.
2 ozs. of Alum.
And 2 ozs. of Copperas.

No. 5.

10 BUNCHES.—LIGHT FIERY BROWN.

Dye with 6 lbs. of Fustic.
$2\frac{1}{2}$ lbs. of Camwood.
3 lbs. of Madder.
8 ozs. of Copperas.

No. 6.

6 GROSS 32s.—MIDDLE OLIVE.

Dye with 16 lbs. of Camwood.
12 lbs. of Fustic.
10 lbs. of Mull Madder.
12 ozs. of Copperas.

———

No. 7.

5 GROSS 32s.—RED LAVENDER.

Dye with 2½ lbs. of Logwood.
8 ozs. of Cudbear.
And 2 ozs. of Alum.

———

No. 8.

6 GROSS 30s.—RED DRAB.

Dye with 1 lb. of Logwood.
4 ozs. of Cudbear.
And 4 ozs. of Alum.

———

No. 9.

12 BUNCHES.—RUBY.

Dye with 2½ lbs. of Cudbear.
If a Blue shade is required, add 1 gill of Ammonia, and if a Red shade, add 1 tot of Spirits.

No. 10.

24 BUNCHES.—WINE COLOR.

Boil it 20 minutes with 4 ozs. of Chrome, and finish it in a clean vessel with 4 lbs. of Cudbear, and 4 ozs. of Logwood. This boiling with Chrome is called Chroming.

No. 11.

24 BUNCHES.—FINE CLARET.

Chrome same as No. 10.
Finish with 2 lbs. of Cudbear.
6 lbs. of Lima Peachwood.

No. 12.

6 GROSS 32s.—YELLOW BROWN.

Dye with 10 lbs. of Camwood.
10 lbs. of Fustic.
8 lbs. of Madder.
8 ozs. of Copperas.

No. 13.

24 BUNCHES, SPUN TO 18 OUNCES.— MIDDLE GREEN.

Dye to middle shade of Blue in the Vat, and fill up with

6 lbs. of Fustic.

2 lbs. of Alum.

1 tot of Chemic.

———

No. 14.

6 GROSS 32s.—GOOD BROWN.

Dye with 20 lbs. of Camwood.

10 lbs. of Madder.

10 lbs. of Fustic.

2 lbs. of Copperas.

———

No. 15.

5 GROSS 32s.—DARK PURPLE.

Boil with 10 lbs. of Alum.

2 lbs. of Argol.

Fill up with 13 lbs. of Logwood.

To dye the shade another way.

Chrome same as No. 10.

Finish with 2 lbs. of Cudbear.

4 lbs. of Logwood.

No. 16.

20 BUNCHES.—SEA GREEN.

Dye with 1 lb. of Alum.
6 lbs. of Fustic.
1 gill of Extract.

———

No. 17.

24 BUNCHES.—DARK BROWN.

Dye with 6 lbs. of Camwood.
12 ozs. of Crop Madder.
1 lb. of Mull Madder.
1 lb. of Fustic.
4 ozs. of Logwood.
And 2 ozs. of Copperas.

———

No. 18.

4 GROSS 32s.—DARK DRAB.

Dye with 1 lb. of Fustic.
8 ozs. of Logwood.
8 ozs. of Madder.
4 ozs. of Camwood.
And 3 ozs. of Copperas.

No. 19.

20 BUNCHES 36s.—MAROON.

Dye with 4 lbs. of Cudbear.
And 1 lb. of Camwood.

No. 20.

20 BUNCHES 36s.—SCARLET.

Dye with 1 lb. of Tartar.
10 ozs. of Young Fustic.
12 ozs. of Cochineal.
1 pint of Spirits.

No. 21.

20 BUNCHES 44s.—CINNAMON BROWN.

Dye with 5 lbs. of Crop Madder.
3 lbs. of Camwood.
2 lbs. of Fustic.
2 ozs. of Alum.
And 1 oz. of Copperas.

No. 22.

20 BUNCHES.—GRAIN CRIMSON.

Dye with 1 lb. of Cochineal.
1 lb. of Tartar.
1 pint of Spirits.

No. 23.
20 BUNCHES.—FULL PINK.

Dye with 4 ozs. of Cochineal.
1 pint of Spirits.
1 lb. of Tartar.

No. 24.
20 BUNCHES.—SALMON COLOR.

Dye with 2 ozs. of Young Fustic.
1 lb. of Tartar.
4 ozs. of Cochineal.
1 pint of Spirits.

No. 25.
20 BUNCHES.—FULL GRAIN ROSE.

Dye with 8 ozs. of Cochineal.
1 lb. of Tartar.
1 pint of Spirits.

No. 26.
20 BUNCHES.—LIGHT BUFF.

Dye with 1 lb. of Tartar.
$\frac{1}{4}$ oz. of Cochineal.
4 ozs. of Fustic.
1 pint of Spirits.

Darker shades may be dyed by adding more
Cochineal, according to shade required.

11

No. 27.

20 BUNCHES.—LIGHT YELLOW.

Dye with 1 lb. of Alum.
1 lb. of Tartar.
2 lbs. of Bark.
2 lbs. of Young Fustic.
3 gills of Spirits.

Fuller shades of Yellow are dyed by adding more Fustic.

No. 28.

20 BUNCHES.—ORANGE.

Dye with 1 lb. of Tartar.
8 ozs. of Cochineal.
1 pint of Spirits.

No. 29.

20 BUNCHES.—BOTTLE GREEN.

After getting a good Blue bottom in the Vat, dye with
1 lb. of Tartar.
2 lbs. of Alum.
10 lbs. of Fustic.
1 gill of Chemic.

No. 30.

20 BUNCHES.—INVISIBLE GREEN.

Chrome same as No. 10, and finish with
4 lbs. of Logwood.
8 lbs. of Fustic.
2 ozs. of Red Argol.

If a Yellower shade is required, add more Fustic, and if darker, more Logwood.

No. 31.

20 BUNCHES.—DARK BLUE.

Chrome same as No. 10, and finish with 5 lbs. of Logwood, and if not Red enough, add a handful of Cudbear.

No. 32.

20 BUNCHES.—BLUE BLACK.

Chrome same as No. 10, and finish with 10 lbs. of Logwood.

No. 33.

20 BUNCHES.—FULL BLACK.

Chrome same as No. 10, and finish with 15 lbs. of Logwood, and 4 lbs. of Fustic.

No. 34.

20 BUNCHES.—ROYAL BLUE.

Dye with 2 lbs. of Prussiate of Potash.
2 quarts of Blue Spirits.

To be entered cold, and heated up as quickly as possible; when boiled 15 minutes, get out, and add

1 quart of finishing Spirits.

Enter again, and boil 15 minutes more.

If a dark shade is required, add a little Logwood with the finishing Spirits.

No. 35.

20 BUNCHES.—APPLE GREEN.

Dye with 8 ozs. of Logwood.
4 lbs. of Fustic.
2 ozs. of Alum.
And 2 ozs. of Copperas.

No. 36.

20 BUNCHES.—LIGHT OLIVE.

Chrome same as No. 10, and finish with
4 lbs. of Fustic.
1 lb. of Logwood.
4 ozs. of Alum.

No. 37.
20 BUNCHES.—DARK OLIVE.

Chrome same as No. 10, and finish with
4 lbs. of Logwood.
6 lbs. of Fustic.
4 ozs. of Alum.

No. 38.
20 BUNCHES.—BROWN OLIVE.

Chrome same as No. 10, and finish with
4 lbs. of Logwood.
6 lbs. of Fustic.
2 lbs. of Camwood, or a little Cudbear,
4 ozs. of Alum.

No. 39.
20 BUNCHES.—FAWN DRAB.

Dye with 1 lb. of Red Argol,
1 lb. of Fustic.
2 ozs. of Cudbear.
½ oz. of Chemic.

No. 40.
10 BUNCHES.—DOVE COLOR.

Dye with 10 ozs. of Brown Tartar.
2 spoonfuls of Chemic.
2 ozs. of Cudbear.

11*

No. 41.

10 BUNCHES.—BLUE LAVENDER.

This shade is dyed with Acid, and not the same as the Red Lavender, No. 7.

Dye with 1 lb. of Tartar.
2 ozs. of Paste Cudbear.
4 ozs. of Chemic.

No. 42.

10 BUNCHES.—SKY BLUE.

Dye with 1 gill of Vitriol.
1 lb. of Red Argol.
1 tot of Liquid Extract.

No. 43.

10 BUNCHES.—SAXON BLUE.

Dye with 1 gill of Oil of Vitriol.
1 lb. of Argol.
1 gill of Liquid Extract.

No. 44.

20 BUNCHES.—SAGE DRAB.

Dye with 2 lbs. of Argol.
1 lb. of Old Fustic.
1 oz. of Chemic.
1 handful of Cudbear.

No. 45.

20 BUNCHES.—CHROMED GREEN.

Chrome same as No. 10, and finish with 4 lbs. of Logwood and 6 lbs. of Fustic.

No. 46.

DARK CHROMED GREEN.

Chrome same as No. 10, and finish with 6 lbs. of Logwood and 10 lbs. of Fustic.

These Greens will much resemble the Greens dyed with Blue bottoms, but are not so permanent.

No. 47.

20 BUNCHES.—LIGHT AND DARK CLARET.

Boil with 10 lbs. of Alum.
2 lbs. of Argol.
Finish with 8 lbs. of Peachwood.
1 lb. of Logwood.

If darker shades are required, add more Logwood.

No. 48.

MOCK CRIMSON.

Boil with 10 lbs. of Alum.

2 lbs. of Argol.

After boiling an hour, wash well, and finish in a clear vessel with 10 lbs. of Peachwood.

1 gill of Spirits.

2 pails of Urine.

Without the Urine it will be a Mock Maroon.

No. 49.

12 BUNCHES.—GRAIN MAROON.

Dye with 1 pint of Spirits.

1½ lb. of Cochineal.

1 lb. of Tartar.

Wash, and in another vessel give it

1 lb. of Cudbear, and wash off.

No. 50.

80 BUNCHES.—DARK CHOCOLATE.

Dye with 35 lbs. of Sanders Wood,

15 lbs. of Fustic.

4 lbs. of Logwood.

4 lbs. of Copperas.

No. 51.

80 BUNCHES.—HEAVY BROWN.

Dye with 20 lbs. of Sanders Wood.
24 lbs. of Fustic.
5 lbs. of Logwood.
4 lbs. of Copperas.

No. 52.

80 BUNCHES.—DARK CLARET BROWN.

Dye with 24 lbs. of Sanders Wood.
4 lbs. of Fustic.
8 lbs. of Logwood.
4 lbs. of Copperas.

No. 53.

80 BUNCHES.—DARKER CLARET BROWN.

Dye with 36 lbs. of Sanders Wood.
8 lbs. of Fustic.
10 lbs. of Logwood.
6 lbs. of Copperas.

No. 54.

100 BUNCHES.—FULL RED BROWN.

Dye with 34 lbs. of Sanders Wood.
15 lbs. of Fustic.
5 lbs. of Logwood.
1 lb. of Red Argol.
6 lbs. of Copperas.

———

No. 55.

50 BUNCHES.—FULL YELLOW BROWN.

Dye with 10 lbs. of Sanders Wood.
24 lbs. of Fustic.
5 lbs. of Logwood.
4 lbs. of Copperas.

———

No. 56.

DARKER YELLOW BROWN.

20 lbs. of Sanders Wood.
40 lbs. of Fustic.
6 lbs. of Logwood.
6 lbs. of Copperas.

No. 57.

50 BUNCHES.—DARK OLIVE.

Dye with 36 lbs. of Fustic.

8 lbs. of Logwood.

2 lbs. of Argol.

2 lbs. of Alum.

2 lbs. of Copperas.

No. 58.

50 BUNCHES.—DARKER SHADE OF OLIVE.

40 lbs. of Fustic.

10 lbs. of Logwood.

2 lbs. of Alum.

2 lbs. of Argol.

4 lbs. of Copperas.

No. 59.

80 BUNCHES.—VERY DARK CLARET.

35 lbs. of Sanders Wood.

20 lbs. of Logwood.

6 lbs. of Copperas.

2 pails of Urine in the saddening.

It is to be understood that where Copperas is used in these Yarns it is for the saddening.

WORSTED YARN DYEING.

No. 1.

80 lbs. OF YARN.—SLATE PURPLE.

Previous to Dyeing, the yarns must be well scoured with Soap and hot Water, at 80°. Then boil twenty minutes with 2 lbs. of Chrome, then wash and finish with 10 lbs. of Logwood, 1 lb. of Cudbear, and boil half an hour, then clean and dry off.

No. 2.

80 lbs. OF YARN.—RED PURPLE.

Prepare same as No. 1, and finish with 10 lbs. of Logwood, and 6 lbs. of Cudbear; boil twenty minutes in the finishing.

No. 3.

80 lbs. OF YARN.—FULL RED PURPLE.

Prepare same as No. 1, and finish with 10 lbs. of Logwood, and 10 lbs. of Cudbear; boil twenty minutes.

No. 4.

80 lbs. OF YARN.—ROYAL BLUE.

6 lbs. of Prussiate, 6 quarts of Blue Spirits, enter cold, and heat up to boiling quickly, and turn them over sharply, after boiling twenty minutes, get out, and add 3 quarts of finishing Spirits. Enter again, and boil a quarter of an hour, get out again, add 3 gills more of finishing Spirits, and 2 lbs. of Logwood. Enter again, and turn them a quarter of an hour very quickly.

For darker shades, add more Logwood, and for lighter, less Logwood.

No. 5.

80 lbs. OF YARN.—GRAIN MAROON.

Boil forty minutes with 8 lbs. of Tartar, 3 quarts of Nitrate of Tin, 5 lbs. Cochineal, then wash in clean water, and finish in a clean vessel with 4 lbs. of Cudbear, and boil a quarter of an hour.

No. 6.

80 lbs. OF YARN.—MOCK CRIMSON.

Boil one hour with 30 lbs. of Alum and 8 lbs. of Argol, then wash well in clean water, and finish in a clean vessel with 30 lbs. of Peachwood, 1 pint of Nitrate of Tin, and 4 quarts of Ammonia.

12

No. 7.

80 lbs. OF YARN.—CLARET.

Boil same as No. 6, and finish with 4 lbs. of Logwood, 30 lbs. of Peachwood.

No. 8.

80 lbs. OF YARN.—LIGHT VICUNA.

Boil half an hour with 3 lbs. of Argol.
1 lb. of Blue Vitriol.
1 lb. of Cudbear.
5 lbs. of Fustic.

No. 9.

80 lbs. OF YARN.—DARK VICUNA.

Boil one hour with 4 lbs. of Argol.
2 lbs. of Blue Vitriol.
2 lbs. of Cudbear.
7 lbs. of Fustic.
7 lbs. of Madder.

No. 10.

80 lbs. OF YARN.—OAK DRAB.

Boil half an hour with 3 lbs. of Argol.
3 lbs. of Blue Vitriol.
20 lbs. of Fustic.
A handful of Cudbear.

No. 11.

80 lbs. OF YARN.—BOTTLE GREEN.

Boil half an hour with 8 lbs. of Red Argol, 2 lbs. of Blue Vitriol, 30 lbs. of Fustic, 4 quarts of Chemic, and 1 lb. of Cudbear.

Most shades of dark Green may be dyed as well with Chrome, which would be a saving of two-thirds of the expense.

No. 12.

80 lbs. OF YARN.—APPLE GREEN.

Boil half an hour with 8 lbs. of Argol.
3 lbs. of Blue Vitriol.
30 lbs. of Fustic.
¾ of a pint of Liquid Extract.

No. 13.

80 lbs. OF YARN.—KNOT GREEN.

Boil half an hour with 8 lbs. of Tartar.
8 lbs. of Alum.
30 lbs. of Fustic.
1 pint of Liquid Extract.

No. 14.

80 lbs. OF YARN.—SEA GREEN.

Boil half an hour with 8 lbs. of Tartar.
2 lbs. of Alum.
5 lbs. of Fustic.
1 gill of Liquid Extract.

———

No. 15.

80 lbs. OF YARN.—DARK SEA GREEN.

Boil half an hour with 8 lbs. of Tartar.
4 lbs. of Alum.
10 lbs. of Fustic.
1 quart of Liquid Extract.

———

No. 16.

80 lbs. OF YARN.—MOCK MAROON.

Boil twenty minutes with 16 lbs. of Cudbear.
1 quart of Nitrate of Tin.

———

No. 17.

80 lbs. OF YARN.—GREEN OLIVE.

Boil half an hour with 8 lbs. of Argol.
3 lbs. of Blue Vitriol.
30 lbs. of Fustic.
1 quart of Liquid Extract.

No. 18.

80 lbs. OF YARN.—DARK OLIVE.

Boil half an hour with 8 lbs. of Argol.
3 lbs. of Blue Vitriol.
30 lbs. of Fustic.
2 quarts of Chemic.
1 lb. of Cudbear.

No. 19.

80 lbs. OF YARN.—DAHLIA.

Boil twenty minutes with 12 lbs. of Cudbear.
1 quart of Ammonia.

No. 20.

80 lbs. OF YARN.—RUBY.

Boil twenty minutes with 12 lbs. of Cudbear.

No. 21.

80 lbs. OF YARN.—APPLE GREEN.

Prepare same as No. 1.
Finish with 3 lbs. of Logwood.
40 lbs. of Fustic.
Boil 20 minutes.

12*

No. 22.

80 lbs. OF YARN.—INVISIBLE GREEN.

Prepare same as No. 1.
Finish with 30 lbs. of Logwood.
30 lbs. of Fustic.
Boil 20 minutes.

———

No. 23.

80 lbs. OF YARN.—BOTTLE GREEN.

Prepare same as No. 1.
Finish with 10 lbs. of Logwood.
25 lbs. of Fustic.
Boil twenty minutes.

———

No. 24.

80 lbs. OF YARN.—BROWN OLIVE.

Boil half an hour with 25 lbs. of Fustic.
20 lbs. of Madder.
Then get the Yarns out of the vessel, and add
2 lbs. of Blue Vitriol.
2 lbs. of Copperas.
Put them in again and turn 20 minutes.

No. 25.

80 lbs. OF YARN.—GREEN OLIVE.

Prepare same as No. 1.
Finish with 6 lbs. of Logwood.
30 lbs. of Fustic.
Boil 20 minutes.

No. 26.

80 lbs. OF YARN.—CANARY COLOR.

Boil half an hour with 5 lbs. of Quercitron Bark.
4 lbs. of Alum.
2 quarts of Spirits.

No. 27.

80 lbs. OF YARN.—FULL YELLOW.

Boil half an hour with 30 lbs. of Young Fustic.
4 lbs. of Tartar.
2 quarts of Spirits.

No. 28.

80 lbs. OF YARN.—ORANGE.

Boil 1 hour with 2 lbs. of Cochineal.
30 lbs. of Young Fustic.
4 lbs. of Tartar.
3 quarts of Spirits.

No. 29.

80 lbs. OF YARN.—GRAIN CRIMSON.

Boil 1 hour with 8 lbs. of Paste Cochineal.
1 lb. of Dry Cochineal.
4 lbs. of Tartar.
2 quarts of Spirits.

———

No. 30.

80 lbs. OF YARN.—ROSE.

Boil 1 hour with 3½ lbs. of Paste Cochineal.
4 lbs. of Tartar.
2 quarts of Spirits.

———

No. 31.

80 lbs. OF YARN.—PINK.

Boil half an hour with 2 lbs. of Paste Cochineal.
4 lbs. of Tartar.
2 quarts of Spirits.

———

To MAKE COCHINEAL PASTE.—Add 3 gills of Strong Ammonia to 1 lb. of Cochineal, and mix it well in a Jar, put the Jar into a Vessel of boiling water, keeping the water out of the Jar, during about 8 hours, or upon a warm Sand-Bath during about 12 hours, or upon a Boiler.

No. 32.

80 lbs. OF YARN.—IMITATION OF INDIGO BLUE.

Prepare same as No. 1.
Finish with 20 lbs. of Logwood.
1 pint of Ammonia.
Boil 20 minutes.

No. 33.

80 lbs. OF YARN.—LIGHT BROWN.

Prepare same as No. 1.
Finish with 30 lbs. of Peachwood.
20 lbs. of Fustic.
Boil 20 minutes.

No. 34.

80 lbs. OF YARN.—CLARET BROWN.

Prepare same as No. 1.
Finish with 30 lbs. of Peachwood.
Boil 20 minutes.

No. 35.

80 lbs. OF YARN.—SNUFF COLOR.

Boil 1 hour with 25 lbs. of Fustic.
20 lbs. of Madder.
2 lbs. of Blue Vitriol.
Boil half an hour.

———

No. 36.

80 lbs. OF YARN.—FULL BLACK.

Prepare same as No. 1.
Finish with 40 lbs. of Logwood.
15 lbs. of Fustic.
Boil 20 minutes.

———

No. 37.

80 lbs. OF YARN.—BLUE BLACK.

Prepare same as No. 1.
Finish with 30 lbs. of Logwood.
Boil 20 minutes.

———

No. 38.

80 lbs. OF YARN.—FAWN DRAB.

Boil half an hour with 8 lbs. of White Argol.
2 lbs. of Fustic.
1 handful of Cudbear.
2 spoonfuls of Chemic.

No. 39.

80 lbs. OF YARN.—LILAC.

Boil half an hour with 8 lbs. of Tartar.
1 lb. of Cudbear.
Half a gill of Liquid Extract.

No. 40.

80 lbs. OF YARN.—LAVENDER.

Boil half an hour with 8 lbs. of Tartar.
1 lb. of Paste Cudbear.
1 pint of Liquid Extract.

No. 41.

80 lbs. OF YARN.—LIGHT PUCE.

Boil 20 minutes with 5 lbs. of Archil.

No. 42.

80 lbs. OF YARN.—SLATE DRAB.

Boil half an hour with 8 lbs. of Argol.
3 lbs. of Fustic.
3 handfuls of Cudbear.
1 gill of Chemic.

No. 43.

80 lbs. OF YARN.—SAGE DRAB.

Boil half an hour with 8 lbs. of Argol.
2 lbs. of Fustic.
2 handfuls of Cudbear.
2 spoonfuls of Chemic.

No. 44.

80 lbs. OF YARN.—RED CINNAMON BROWN.

Boil 2 hours with 40 lbs. of Camwood, or Red Sanders.
No Saddening.

No. 45.

80 lbs. OF YARN.—DARK BROWN.

Boil same as the last.
Sadden with 1 lb. of Blue Vitriol.
3 lbs. of Copperas.

Turn them on half an hour without boiling.

No. 46.

80 lbs. OF YARN.—DARK RED BROWN.

Boil same as No. 44.
Sadden with 4 lbs. of Copperas.

No. 47.

80 lbs. OF YARN.—GRAIN SCARLET.

Boil 1 hour with 5 lbs. of Cochineal.
20 lbs. of Young Fustic.
7 lbs. of White or Brown Tartar.
3 quarts of Nitrate of Tin, or Oxalic Muriate of
Tin, which is preferable.

———

No. 48.

80 lbs. OF YARN.—SALMON.

Boil half an hour with 12 ounces of Dry Cochineal.
4 lbs. of Tartar.
2 quarts of Spirits.

———

No. 49.

80 lbs. OF YARN.—SKY BLUE.

Boil half an hour with 8 lbs. of Tartar.
1 gill of Liquid Extract.

———

No. 50.

80 lbs. OF YARN.—SAXON BLUE.

Boil half an hour with 1 pint of Liquid Extract.
8 lbs. of Tartar.

13

No. 51.

80 lbs. OF YARN.—DOVE COLOR.

Boil half an hour with 8 lbs. of Tartar.
1 gill of Extract.
1 lb. of Paste Cudbear.

Brighter shades of this color may be got by adding Paste Cochineal instead of Cudbear, but to brighten Cudbear, run through a little Ammonia and warm Water.

WOOLLEN-DYEING.

No. 1.

**2 *Pieces*, LONGWOOLS, 80 lbs. each.—
GRAIN SCARLET.**

Boil 1 hour with 9 lbs. of Young Fustic, 6 lbs. of
Tartar.

6 quarts of Spirits; finish in a clean vessel with
4½ lbs. of Lac, 4½ lbs. of Cochineal, 4 quarts
of Spirits, besides the 6 pints mixed with the
Lac. Boil 1 hour.

☞ The Spirit to be used is Nitrate of Tin,
or two parts of Nitrate of Tin, and one part of
Oxalic Muriate of Tin, which is preferable.

No. 2.

4 *Pieces*, BOCKINS, 36 lbs. each.—SCARLET.

Boil 1¼ hour with 12 lbs. of Lac, 10 lbs. of Young
Fustic, 6 lbs. of Tartar, and 13 quarts of Spirits.

No. 3.

4 *Pieces*, ORANGE LISTS, 35 lbs. each.— SCARLET.

Dye with 10 lbs. of good Lac.
6 lbs. of Young Fustic.
6 lbs. of Brown Tartar.
3 gallons of Spirits.

> Boil 1¼ hour.

———

No. 4.

2 *Pieces*, SAVED LISTS, 70 lbs. each.— SCARLET.

Dye with 10 lbs. of Lac.
6 lbs. of Tartar.
8 lbs. of Young Fustic.
3 gallons of Spirits.

> Boil 1¼ hour.

———

No. 5.

2 *Pieces*, LONGWOOLS, 75 lbs. each.—LAC SCARLET.

Dye with 12 lbs. of Lac.
8 lbs. of Tartar.
2 lbs. of Rasped Fustic.
9 quarts of Spirits.

> Boil 1¼ hour.

No. 6.

20 *Pieces*, SERGES, 8 lbs. each.—SCARLET.

Dye with 20 lbs. of Lac.
12 lbs. of Tartar.
10 lbs. of Young Fustic.
12 quarts of Spirits.

Boil 1 hour.

No. 7.

6 *Ends*, FINE SAVED LISTS, 20 lbs. each.—
SCARLET.

Dye with 14 lbs. of Lac.
7 lbs. of Young Fustic.
8 lbs. of Tartar.
6 quarts of Spirits.

Boil 1½ hour.

No. 8.

4 *Pieces*, GOLD LISTS, 40 lbs. each.—
ORANGE.

Dye with 2 lbs. of Cochineal.
12 lbs. of Quercitron Bark.
½ lb. of Lac.
6 lbs. of Tartar.
12 pints of Bark Spirits.

Boil 1 hour.

13*

No. 9.

2 *Ends*, BOCKINS, 68 lbs. each.—SALMON.

Dye with ½ lb. of Cochineal.
¼ lb. of Paste Cochineal.
4 lbs. of Tartar.
1 lb. of Fustic.
12 pints of Spirits.
Boil 1 hour.

———

No. 10.

4 *Pieces*, ORANGE LISTS, 35 lbs. each.—
SALMON.

Dye with 2½ lbs. of Cochineal.
4 lbs. of Rasped Fustic.
4 lbs. of Tartar.
7 quarts of Spirits.
Boil 1 hour.

———

No. 11.

2 *Pieces*, LONGWOOLS, 80 lbs. each.—
GRAIN-ROSE.

Dye with 4 lbs. of Cochineal.
4 lbs. of Tartar.
13 pints of Spirits.

Blue up-in a cistern of warm water, with Urine according to shade required.

No. 12.

4 *Pieces*, ORANGE LISTS, 34 lbs. each.—
GOLD COLOR.

Boil 1 hour with 2 lbs. of Cochineal.
12 ozs. of Lac.
13 lbs. of Quercitron Bark.
12 lbs. of Bark Spirits.

Boil 1 hour.

———

No. 13.

6 *Ends*, ORANGE LISTS, 28 lbs. each.—
GRAIN-ROSE.

5½ lbs. of Cochineal.
7 lbs. of Tartar.
9 quarts of Spirits.
Blue as No. 11.

Boil 1 hour.

———

No. 14.

3 *Pieces*, SAVED LISTS, 58 lbs. each.—
FULL RED CRIMSON.

Dye with 4 lbs. of Lac.
1½ lb. of Dry Cochineal.
7 lbs. of Paste Cochineal.
7 lbs. of Brown Tartar.
10 quarts of Spirits.

Boil 1 hour.

No. 15.

4 *Pieces*, ORANGE LISTS, 34 lbs. each.— LIGHT ROSE.

Dye with 2½ lbs. of Cochineal.
2 lbs. of Alum.
6 lbs. of Tartar.
6 quarts of Spirits.

No. 16.

2 *Pieces*, LONGWOOLS, 80 lbs. each.— ROSE COLOR.

6 lbs. of Tartar.
2 lbs. of Alum.
6 quarts of Spirits.

Boil 1 hour.

List them over a Horse-tree, without washing, till
next day; then finish with
½ lb. of Paste Cochineal.
2½ lbs. of Dry Cochineal.
3 pints of Spirits.

No. 17.

4 *Ends*, LITTLE BOCKINS, 25 lbs. each.— YELLOW.

Dye with 4 lbs. of Tartar.
12 lbs. of Young Fustic.
7 quarts of Spirits.

Boil half an hour.

No. 18.

6 *Ends*, GOLD LISTS, 34 lbs. each.—FULL YELLOW, OR AMBER.

Dye with 12 lbs. of Quercitron Bark.
12 lbs. of Fustic.
7 lbs. of Tartar.
5 quarts of Spirits.
Boil half an hour.

———

No. 19.

4 *Pieces*, ORANGE LISTS, 30 lbs. each.— SKY BLUE.

Dye with 10 lbs. of Crystals.
10 lbs. of Alum.
2 quarts of Oil of Vitriol.
3gill s of Liquid Extract.
Boil half an hour.

———

No. 20.

4 *Ends*, GOLD LISTS, 30 lbs. each.—DOVE COLOR.

Dye with 1 lb. of Paste Cochineal.
8 lbs. of Tartar.
10 spoonfuls of Liquid Extract.
Boil 40 minutes.

No. 21.

2 *Pieces*, BROADCLOTHS, 42 Yards each.—
CRIMSON.

Dye with 3 lbs. of Lac.
4½ lbs. of Cochineal.
6 quarts of Spirits.
Clean and blue in a cistern of warm water with
5 lbs. of Cudbear.
8 pails of Urine.

___

No. 22.

20 *Pieces*, SERGES, 8 lbs. each.—GREEN.

Dye with 40 lbs. of Fustic.
4 pints of Chemic.
4 lbs. of Argol.
8 lbs. of Alum.

Boil 1 hour,

___

No. 23.

4 *Ends*, CLOTH, 24 lbs. each.—ROYAL
BLUE.

Dye with 6 lbs. of Prussiate.
6 quarts of Royal Blue Spirits.

Enter cold and heat up quickly, and turn on
sharply, after boiling 20 minutes get out, and add
2 quarts of Finishing Spirits, enter again, and
boil 20 minutes.

No. 24.

4 *Ends*, 24 lbs. each.—DARK ROYAL BLUE.

Dye with 6 lbs. of Prussiate.
6 quarts of Royal Blue Spirits.

Enter cold and heat up quickly, and turn on sharply; after boiling 20 minutes, get out, and add 2 quarts of Finishing Spirits; enter again, and boil 20 minutes; get out, and cool over, then add 2 lbs. of Logwood, and 1 quart of Finishing Spirits. Boil 20 minutes.

No. 25.

10 *Pieces*, SERGES, 8 lbs. each.—ROYAL BLUE.

Dye with 8 lbs. of Prussiate.
8 quarts of Royal Blue Spirits.
3 quarts of Finishing Spirits.
Logwood according to shade required.
Heat up same as No. 23.

No. 26.

4 *Pieces*, ORANGE LISTS, 34 lbs. each.— ROYAL BLUE.

Dye with 6 lbs. of Prussiate.
6 quarts of Royal Blue Spirits.
3 quarts of Finishing Spirits.
1, 2, 8, or 4 lbs. of Logwood, according to shade.

No. 27.

2 *Pieces*, LONGWOOLS, 80 lbs. each.— ROYAL BLUE.

Dye with 6 lbs. of Prussiate.
12 pints of Royal Blue Spirits.
6 pints of Finishing Spirits.
Logwood according to shade.
Heat same as No. 24.

———

No. 28.

Gold Lists are dyed in all respects as No. 26.

———

No. 29.

2 *Pieces*, LONGWOOLS, 80 lbs. each.— GREEN.

Dye with 60 lbs. of Fustic.
1 pint of Chemic.
10 lbs. of Alum.
10 lbs. of Argol.

Boil 1 hour.

No. 30.

4 *Ends*, LADIES' CLOTHS, 25 yards each.—
PURPLE.

Boil 2½ hours with 40 lbs. of Alum.

8 lbs. of Argol.

1 quart of Nitrate of Tin.

Wash well and finish with 30 lbs. of Logwood, and
4 lbs. of Peachwood, in a clean vessel.

Enter cool in the finishing, and heat up to the
boiling point.

No. 31.

4 *Pieces*, PILOT CLOTHS, 120 lbs. each.—
DARK BROWN.

Stuff with 40 lbs. of Fustic.

40 lbs. of Sanders.

6 lbs. of Logwood.

Sadden with 6 lbs. of Copperas.

No. 32.

8 *Ends*, NARROW HONLEYS, 40 yards
each.—DARK CLARET BROWN.

Stuff with 70 lbs. of Sanders.

10 lbs. of Fustic.

6 lbs. of Logwood.

Sadden with 8 lbs. of Copperas.

1 cupful of Oil of Vitriol.

14

No. 33.

1 *Piece*, FLUSHING, 112 lbs.—BLACK.

Stuff with 10 lbs. of Copperas.
3 lbs. of Blue Vitriol.
3 lbs. of Argol.
2 lbs. of Sumach.
2 lbs. of Fustic.
Finish with 30 lbs. of Logwood.

Boil 1 hour.

——

To Dye the same with Chrome :—

Boil half an hour with 1 lb. of Chrome.
½ lb. of Red Argol.
Wash well, and then finish with 24 lbs. of Logwood.

Boil 40 minutes.

——

No. 34.

12 *Ends*, BOCKINS.—PEACHWOOD RED.

Boil 3 hours with 60 lbs. of Alum.
20 lbs. of Red Argol.
Finish in a pan, 4 at a time, with 40 lbs. of solid
Peachwood. ·
1 gill of Nitrate of Tin.
For Bluer shades add a little Urine.

No. 35.

2 *Pieces*, LONGWOOLS, 80 lbs. each.—
GREEN.

Dye with 3 lbs. of Tartar.
10 lbs. of Alum.
3 gills of Chemic.
20 lbs. of Fustic.

Boil 1 hour.

No. 36.

2 *Pieces*, LONGWOOLS, 80 lbs. each.—
CHESTNUT BROWN.

Stuff with 120 lbs. of Sanders.
16 lbs. of Fustic.
In the middle of the saddening, add a pint of Oil
of Vitriol.
Sadden with $\frac{1}{2}$ lb. of Copperas.

No. 37.

3 *Pieces*, BROADCLOTHS.—DARK
GREEN.

Dye with 10 lbs. of Argol.
6 lbs. of Madder.
5 pints of Chemic.
40 lbs. of Fustic.

Boil 2 hours.

No. 38.

3 *Pieces*, LONGWOOLS, 80 lbs. each.— CLARET BROWN.

Stuff with 60 lbs. of Sanders.
30 lbs. of Fustic.
5 lbs. of Logwood.
Sadden with 3 lbs. of Copperas.

No. 39.

4 *Pieces*, LADIES' CLOTH.—CHROMED GREEN.

Boil half an hour with 1 lb. of Chrome.
Finish with 20 lbs. of Fustic.
10 lbs. of Logwood.
    Boil half an hour in the finishing.

No. 40.

2 *Pieces*, BOCKINS, 40 lbs. each.— CLARET.

Stuff with 30 lbs. of Sanders.
6 lbs. of Logwood.
Sadden with 6 lbs. of Copperas.
2 pailfuls of Urine.

Lighter or Darker Shades may be got by giving more or less Logwood in the Stuffing, and more or less Copperas in the Saddening.

No. 41.

2 *Pieces*, LADIES' CLOTH.—BROWN OLIVE.

Stuff with 30 lbs. of Fustic.
6 lbs. of Logwood.
3 lbs. of Sanders.
Sadden with 4 lbs. of Copperas.

———

No. 42.

2 *Pieces*, FLUSHINGS, 100 lbs. each.— MULE DRAB.

Dye in the Grease, stuff with 14 lbs. of Camwood.
1 lb. of Fustic.
4 lbs. of Sumach.
24 lbs. of Madder.
Sadden with 6 lbs. of Copperas.

———

No. 43.

2 *Pieces*, FLUSHINGS, 100 lbs. each.— STONE DRAB.

Dye in the Grease, with 20 lbs. of Madder.
1 lb. of Logwood.
1 lb. of Cudbear.
2 lbs. of Sumach.
1 lb. of Copperas,

14*

No. 44.

2 *Pieces*, FLUSHINGS.—FAWN DRAB.

Dye with 6 lbs. of Madder.
2 lbs. of Camwood.
2 handfuls of Fustic.
2 handfuls of Cudbear.
4 ounces of Copperas.

No. 45.

TO DYE 10 STONES OF WOOL NUT BROWN.

Stuff with 60 lbs. of Fustic.
20 lbs. of Sanders.
Add 1 cup of Oil of Vitriol in the middle of the stuffing.
Then sadden with 4 lbs. of Copperas.

No. 46.

TO DYE 4 DRUGGETS, 70 lbs. each, A GOOD LIGHT CLARET.

Boil 3 hours with 60 lbs. of Alum.
10 lbs. of Argol.
1 pint of Nitrate of Tin.
3 lbs. of Logwood.
Finish with 40 lbs. of Lima Peachwood.

No. 47.

TO DYE 4 DRUGGETS A GOOD CRIMSON.

Boil 3 hours with 60 lbs. of Alum.
10 lbs. of Argol.
1 pint of Nitrate of Tin.
Clean, and finish with solid Peachwood, and a little Ammonia, according to shade.

No. 48.

TO DYE 2 PIECES, BOCKINS, 40 lbs. each, A GOOD LOGWOOD BLUE.

Boil with 10 lbs. of Alum.
5 lbs. of Argol.
1 quart of Oil of Vitriol.
Finish with 16 lbs. of Logwood.
3 pails of Urine.

No. 49.

TO DYE 4 PIECES, FLUSHINGS, LOG-WOOD BLUE.

Boil 2 hours with 3 lbs. of Blue Vitriol.

3 lbs. of Red Argol.

3 gills of Oil of Vitriol.

20 lbs. of Alum.

Then clean and finish with 20 lbs. of Chipped Logwood.

4 pails of Urine.

Enter at 150°, and heat up to the boiling point.

This is a good mode of dyeing Logwood Blues.

No. 50.

Wools are prepared the same way, and dyed with the same ingredients, weight for weight, as Yarns and Woollen Pieces are.

No. 51.

NEW MODE OF DYEING LOGWOOD BLUES.

2 *Pieces*, WOOLLEN CLOTHS, 200 lbs. each.—OF ANY QUALITY.

Boil half an hour with 1 lb. of Chrome.

4 lbs. of Alum.

1 lb. of Red Argol.

Clean and finish with 35 lbs. of Logwood.

Boil half an hour in the finishing.

This is the best mode of dyeing a Logwood Blue. It will bear exposure to the atmosphere almost as well as Indigo Blue.

—

No. 52.

2 *Pieces*, BOCKINS, 40 lbs. each.—
MAROON.

Boil 3 hours with 30 lbs. of Alum.
5 lbs. of Red Argol.
1 lb. of Logwood.
Clean and finish with 30 lbs. of Peachwood.
6 pails of Urine.

DAMASK-DYEING.

No. 1.

10 *Pieces*, ¾ COTTON AND WORSTED DAMASKS.—PINK AND WHITE.

Dye in a clean vessel with 10 ozs. of Paste Cochineal.

5 lbs. of Alum.

2 lbs. of White Tartar.

4 pints of Nitrate of Tin.

Boil 30 minutes.

No. 2.

10 *Pieces*, ¾ WORSTED DAMASK.—PINK.

Dye in a clean vessel with 1¼ lb. of Paste Cochineal.

4 lbs. of Alum.

4 lbs. of White Tartar.

6 pints of Nitrate of Tin.

Boil 1 hour.

Lighter or darker shades may be dyed by adding more or less Paste with the same quantity of Acid.

No. 3.

10 *Pieces*, ¾ COTTON AND WORSTED DAMASK.—SALMON AND WHITE.

Dye in a clean vessel with 4 ozs. of Dry Cochineal.

5 lbs. of Brown Tartar.

5 pints of Nitrate of Tin.

Boil 50 minutes.

No. 4.

10 *Pieces*, ¾ WORSTED DAMASK.— SALMON.

Dye in a clean vessel with 8 ozs. of Dry Cochineal.

10 pints of Nitrate of Tin.

6 lbs. of Tartar.

Boil 1 hour.

If a Yellower shade is required, add 4 ozs. of Ground Fustic.

No. 5.

10 *Pieces*, ¾ COTTON AND WORSTED DAMASKS.—ROSE COLOR.

Dye in a clean vessel with 1 lb. of Dry Cochineal.

4 lbs. of Brown Tartar.

2 lbs. of Alum.

6 pints of Nitrate of Tin.

Boil 40 minutes.

No. 6.

10 *Pieces*, ¾ WORSTED DAMASKS.—ROSE COLOR.

Dye in a clean vessel with 1½ lb. of Dry Cochineal.
5 lbs. of Brown Tartar.
4 quarts of Nitrate of Tin.
Boil 1 hour.

If Bluer shades are required, let one-half of the Cochineal be paste, and the other half dry, and rather less Nitrate of Tin.

No. 7.

10 *Pieces*, COTTON AND WORSTED DA-MASKS. — WHITE AND LIGHT RED CRIMSON.

Dye in a clean vessel with 2 lbs. of Alum.
4 lbs. of Brown Tartar.
1½ lb. of Dry Cochineal.
4 quarts of Nitrate of Tin.
Boil 40 minutes.

No. 8.

10 *Pieces,* ¾ WORSTED DAMASKS.— LIGHT RED CRIMSON.

Dye in a clean vessel with 4 lbs. of Alum.
6 lbs. of Brown Tartar.
2½ lbs. of Dry Cochineal.
10 pints of Nitrate of Tin.
Boil 1 hour.

No. 9.

10 *Pieces,* COTTON AND WORSTED DAMASKS.—GRAIN CRIMSON.

Dye in a clean vessel with 4 lbs. of Paste Cochineal.
2 lbs. of Dry Cochineal.
2 lbs. of Alum.
4 lbs. of Brown Tartar.
10 pints of Nitrate of Tin.
Boil 40 minutes.

15

No. 10.

10 *Pieces*, ¾ WORSTED DAMASK.—GRAIN CRIMSON.

Dye in a clean vessel with 5 lbs. of Paste Cochineal.

2½ lbs. of Dry Cochineal.

5 lbs. of Brown Tartar.

3 lbs. of Alum.

6 quarts of Nitrate of Tin.

Boil 1 hour.

When the shades are not required very blue, more Dry Cochineal must be used, and less Paste Cochineal, and if wanted Bluer, use more Paste Cochineal, and less Dry Cochineal.

———

No. 11.

10 *Pieces*, ¾ DAMASK COTTON AND WORSTED.—BUFF AND WHITE.

Dye in a clean vessel with 2 ozs. of Dry Cochineal.

1 lb. of Young Fustic.

4 lbs. of Tartar.

6 pints of Nitrate of Tin.

Boil 40 minutes.

No. 12.

10 *Pieces*, WORSTED DAMASKS.—BUFF.

Dye in a clean vessel with 3 ozs. of Dry Cochineal.

1½ lb. of Young Fustic.

6 lbs. of Tartar.

8 pints of Nitrate of Tin.

Darker shades may be dyed by adding more Cochineal, and the same quantity of other ingredients.

No. 13.

10 *Pieces*, ¾ COTTON AND WORSTED
DAMASKS.—STRAW COLOR
AND WHITE.

Dye in a clean vessel with 5 lbs. of Brown Tartar.

10 ozs. of Young Fustic.

1 oz. of Dry Cochineal.

6 pints of Nitrate of Tin.

Boil 20 minutes.

No. 14.

10 *Pieces*, ¾ WORSTED DAMASKS.—
STRAW COLOR.

Dye in a clean vessel with 6 lbs. of Brown Tartar.

12 ozs. of Young Fustic.

1½ oz. of Dry Cochineal.

8 pints of Nitrate of Tin.

Boil 40 minutes.

No. 15.

10 *Pieces*, ¾ COTTON AND WORSTED DAMASKS.—YELLOW AND WHITE.

Dye in a clean vessel with 5 lbs. of Brown Tartar.
5 lbs. of Young Fustic.
5 pints of Nitrate of Tin.
Boil 20 minutes.

No. 16.

10 *Pieces*, ¾ DAMASKS.—YELLOW.

Dye in a clean vessel with 6 lbs. of Brown Tartar.
6 lbs. of Young Fustic.
8 pints of Nitrate of Tin.
Boil half an hour.

Darker shades of Yellow may be dyed by adding more Fustic, and using the same quantity of the other ingredients. If very bright shades are required, use more Spirits in the dyeing.

No. 17.

10 *Pieces*, ¾ COTTON AND WORSTED DAMASK.—LAC SCARLET AND WHITE.

Dye in a clean vessel with 7 lbs. of Lac.
5 lbs. of Young Fustic.
8 pints of Nitrate of Tin.
5 lbs. of Brown Tartar or White Argol.
Boil 1 hour.

No. 18.

10 *Pieces*, ¾ WORSTED DAMASKS.—LAC
SCARLET.

Dye in a clean vessel with 6 lbs. of White Argol.
6 lbs. of Young Fustic.
10 pints of Nitrate of Tin.
8 lbs. of Lac.

Boil 1 hour.

—

No. 19,

10 *Pieces*, ¾ COTTON AND WORSTED
DAMASKS.—GRAIN SCARLET
AND WHITE.

Dye in a clean vessel with 5 lbs. of Dry Cochineal.
5 lbs. of Brown Tartar.
2½ lbs. of Young Fustic.
8 pints of Nitrate of Tin.

Boil 1 hour.

15*

No. 20.

10 *Pieces*, WORSTED DAMASKS.—GRAIN SCARLET.

Dye with 6 lbs. of Dry Cochineal.
6 lbs. of Brown Tartar.
10 pints of Nitrate of Tin.
2½ lbs. of Young Fustic.
Boil 1 hour.

This is the real Grain Scarlet. It can be imitated with Lac Dye, but is not quite so bright.

No. 21.

10 *Pieces*, ¾ COTTON AND WORSTED DAMASKS.—LIGHT ORANGE AND WHITE.

Dye in a clean vessel with 5 lbs. of Brown Tartar.
6 pints of Nitrate of Tin.
6 lbs. of Young Fustic.
12 ozs. of Dry Cochineal.
Boil 40 minutes.

No. 22.

10 *Pieces*, ¾ WORSTED DAMASKS.— ORANGE.

Dye in a clean vessel with 7 lbs. of Brown Tartar.
8 pints of Nitrate of Tin.
10 lbs. of Young Fustic.
1½ lb. of Cochineal.

Boil 1 hour.

When Yellower shades are wanted, use more Fustic, and when Redder shades are wanted, use more Cochineal, with the same quantity of Spirits and Tartar.

No. 23.

10 *Pieces*, ¾ COTTON AND WORSTED DA-MASKS.—SKY BLUE AND WHITE.

Dye in a clean vessel with 20 lbs. of Common Crystals.
3 pints of Oil of Vitriol.
¾ of a pint of Liquid Extract.
2 spoonfuls of Nitrate of Tin.
1 oz. of Prussiate of Potash.

Boil 40 minutes.

No. 24.

10 *Pieces*, ¾ WORSTED DAMASKS.—SKY
BLUE.

Dye in a clean vessel with 2 quarts of Oil of
Vitriol.
20 lbs. of Crystals.
1 tot of Nitrate of Tin.
1 pint of Liquid Extract.
2 ozs. of Prussiate of Potash.

The Prussiate will give the color a bloomy appearance, which is difficult to get without it.

No. 25.

10 *Pieces*, ¾ COTTON AND WORSTED
DAMASKS.—SAXON BLUE
AND WHITE.

Dye in a clean vessel with 20 lbs. of Crystals.
2 quarts of Oil of Vitriol.
2 ozs. of Prussiate.
1 tot of Nitrate of Tin.
1 pint of Liquid Extract.
Boil 1 hour.

No. 26.

10 *Pieces*, ¾ WORSTED DAMASKS.— SAXON BLUE.

Dye in a clean vessel with 20 lbs. of Crystals.
2 quarts of Oil of Vitriol.
4 ozs. of Prussiate.
1 tot of Nitrate of Tin.
3 gills of Liquid Extract.

> Boil 1 hour.

If Darker shades are required, add more Liquid Extract, according to shade.

———

No. 27.

10 *Pieces*, ¾ COTTON AND WORSTED DAMASKS.—LIGHT GREEN AND WHITE.

Dye in a clean vessel with 15 lbs. of Alum.
6 lbs. of White Argol.
15 lbs. of Chipped Fustic.
1 tot of Liquid Extract.

> Boil 1 hour.

No. 28.

10 *Pieces*, ¾ WORSTED DAMASKS.— LIGHT GREEN.

Dye with 20 lbs. of Alum.
20 lbs. of Fustic.
8 lbs. of White Argol.
1½ tot of Liquid Extract.

Boil 1 hour.

If the shade is required Bluer, add a little more Extract, and if Yellower, a little more Fustic.

———

No. 29.

10 *Pieces*, ¾ COTTON AND WORSTED DAMASKS.—MIDDLE GREEN AND WHITE.

Dye in a clean vessel with 6 lbs. of White Argol.
15 lbs. of Alum.
1 gill of Chemic.
20 lbs. of Fustic.

Boil 1 hour.

No. 30.

10 *Pieces*, ¾ WORSTED DAMASKS.— MIDDLE GREEN.

Dye with 6 lbs. of White Argol.
20 lbs. of Alum.
¾ pint of Chemic.
25 lbs. of Fustic.

Boil 1 hour.

Darker shades of Green must have more Chemic, and if a Yellower shade is required, add more Fustic.

———

No. 31.

10 *Pieces*, ¾ COTTON AND WORSTED DAMASKS.—CINNAMON BROWN AND WHITE.

Dye in a clean vessel with 40 lbs. of Old Rasped Fustic.
2 lbs. of Camwood.
10 lbs. of Super Argol.
2 lbs. of Red Argol.
20 lbs. of Alum.
10 lbs. of Madder.

No. 32.

10 *Pieces*, ¾ WORSTED DAMASKS.— CINNAMON BROWN.

Dye with 50 lbs. of Old Rasped Fustic.
15 lbs. of Super Argol.
25 lbs. of Alum.
4 lbs. of Red Argol.

2½ lbs. of Camwood, or a handful of Cudbear may be used in the place of Camwood, which will produce the same effect.

Boil 1½ hour.

If a flatter shade is required, add a spoonful of Liquid Extract.

No. 33.

15 *Pieces*, ¾ COTTON AND WORSTED DAMASKS.—LIGHT FAWN.

Dye in a clean vessel with 10 lbs. of Super Argol.
1 quart of Oil of Vitriol.
2 handfuls of Madder.
The size of a Knor of Paste Cudbear.
1 spoonful of Liquid Extract.

Boil 1 hour.

No. 34.

15 *Pieces*, ¾ WORSTED DAMASKS.— DARKER FAWN.

Dye in a clean vessel with 10 lbs. of Super Argol.
1 quart of Oil of Vitriol.
2 spoonfuls of Liquid Extract.
4 handfuls of Madder.
1 handful of Paste Cudbear.
Boil to shade.

If a darker shade is required, add more Extract.

No. 35.

10 *Pieces*, ¾ DAMASKS.—LIGHT SILVER DRAB.

Dye in a clean vessel with 10 lbs. of Super Argol.
1 quart of Oil of Vitriol.
1 handful of Paste Cudbear.
2 spoonfuls of Liquid Extract.
Boil 40 minutes.

16

No. 36.

10 *Pieces*, DAMASKS.—DARKER SILVER DRAB.

Dye in a clean vessel with 10 lbs. of Super Argol.
1 quart of Oil of Vitriol.
2 handfuls of Cudbear.
1 handful of Madder.
4 spoonfuls of Liquid Extract.
Boil 1 hour.

If a darker shade is required, add more Liquid Extract, and other ingredients.

No. 37.

10 *Pieces*, ¼ WORSTED DAMASKS.— MOCK CRIMSON.

The Pieces must be boiled for 3 hours in a clean vessel with 30 lbs. of Alum.
10 lbs. of White Argol or Brown Tartar.
1 quart of Nitrate of Tin.

After which, they must be well cleaned, and then they must be finished in another clean vessel with

25 lbs. of Peachwood.
3 gills of Nitrate of Tin.
5 pailfuls of Urine.

Boil a few Ends. Then clean and dry for the press.

This color will very much approach the Grain Crimson, but will not so well bear exposure to the atmosphere.

The Cotton and Worsted Damasks are dyed the same way, but require less Acid in the boiling and less Peachwood in the finishing. In dyeing this color, the Cotton is sometimes bleached, which tends to improve it very much.

It must be passed a few times through a weak Chloride of Lime Liquor, with a little Nitric Acid in it. Sulphuric Acid is too strong, and affects the color too much. The Pieces should next be cleaned, and then blued up to pattern in a vessel of warm water, with Urine according to the shade required.

———

No. 38.

10 *Pieces*, ¾ DAMASK.—SEA GREEN.

Dye in a clean vessel, at boiling heat, with 5 lbs. of Fustic.

1 tot of Liquid Extract.

20 lbs. of Alum.

5 lbs. of White Argol.

Boil 1 hour.

When the shade is required darker, add more Extract, and if Yellower, add more Fustic.

No. 39.

10 *Pieces*, ¾ DAMASKS.—COFFEE BROWN.

Dye with 30 lbs. of Camwood.
10 lbs. of Red Argol, or 20 lbs. of Super Argol.
1 pint of Chemic.
3 pints of Oil of Vitriol.

Boil 2 hours.

This shade of Color is not often wanted, but as it
is sometimes called for, it is here inserted.

No. 40.

10 *Pieces*, DAMASKS.—BLACK.

Boil the pieces 40 minutes in a clean vessel with
2 lbs. of Red Argol.
1 lb. of Chrome.

Wash them and finish in another vessel with
20 lbs. of Logwood.
5 lbs. of Old Fustic.

Boil half an hour.

MOREEN-DYEING.

No. 1.

15 *Pieces*, ¾ MOREENS.—LIGHT SKY BLUE.

Dye in a clean vessel with 20 lbs. of Common Crystals.

3 pints of Oil of Vitriol.

¾ of a pint of Liquid Extract.

2 spoonfuls of Nitrate of Tin.

1 oz. of Prussiate of Potash.

Boil 40 minutes.

No. 2.

15 *Pieces*, ¾ MOREENS.—DARK SKY BLUE.

Dye in a clean vessel with 2 quarts of Oil of Vitriol.

20 lbs. of Crystals.

1 tot of Nitrate of Tin.

1 pint of Liquid Extract.

2 ozs. of Prussiate of Potash.

The Prussiate will give the color a bloomy appearance, which is difficult to get without it.

16*

No. 3.

15 *Pieces*, ¾ MOREENS.—FULL ORANGE.

Dye in a clean vessel with 7 lbs. of Brown Tartar.
8 pints of Nitrate of Tin.
10 lbs. of Young Fustic.
1½ lb. of Cochineal.

Boil 1 hour.

When Yellower shades are wanted, use more Fustic, and when Redder shades are wanted, use more Cochineal, with the same quantity of Spirits and Tartar.

———

No. 4.

15 *Pieces*, ¾ MOREENS.—LIGHT ORANGE.

Dye in a clean vessel with 5 lbs. of Brown Tartar.
6 pints of Nitrate of Tin.
6 lbs. of Young Fustic.
12 ozs. of Dry Cochineal.

Boil 40 minutes.

No. 5.

15 *Pieces*, MOREENS.—FULL GRAIN SCARLET.

Dye with 6 lbs. of Dry Cochineal.

6 lbs. of Brown Tartar.

10 pints of Nitrate of Tin.

2½ lbs. of Young Fustic.

Boil 1 hour.

This is the real Grain Scarlet. It can be imitated with Lac Dye, but it is not quite so bright.

No. 6.

15 *Pieces*, ¾ MOREENS.—GRAIN SCARLET.

Dye in a clean vessel with 5 lbs. of Dry Cochineal.

5 lbs. of Brown Tartar.

2½ lbs. of Young Fustic.

8 pints of Nitrate of Tin.

Boil 1 hour.

No. 7.

15 *Pieces*, ¾ MOREENS.—LIGHT LAC SCARLET.

Dye in a clean vessel with 6 lbs. of White Argol.

6 lbs. of Young Fustic.

10 pints of Nitrate of Tin.

8 lbs. of Lac.

Boil 1 hour.

No. 8.

15 *Pieces*, ¾ MOREENS.—FULL LAC SCARLET.

Dye in a clean vessel with 10 lbs. of Lac.
5 lbs. of Young Fustic.
10 pints of Nitrate of Tin.
7 lbs. of Brown Tartar or White Argol.
Boil 1 hour.

No. 9.

15 *Pieces*, ¾ MOREENS.—LIGHT YELLOW.

Dye in a clean vessel with 5 lbs. of Brown Tartar.
5 lbs. of Young Fustic.
5 pints of Nitrate of Tin.
Boil 20 minutes.

No. 10.

15 *Pieces*, ¾ MOREENS.—FULL YELLOW.

Dye in a clean vessel with 6 lbs. of Brown Tartar.
10 lbs. of Young Fustic.
8 pints of Nitrate of Tin.
Boil half an hour.

Darker shades of Yellow may be dyed by adding more Fustic, and using the same quantity of the other ingredients. If very bright shades are required, use more Nitrate of Tin in the dyeing.

No. 11.

15 *Pieces*, ¾ MOREENS.—STRAW COLOR.

Dye in a clean vessel with 5 lbs. of Brown Tartar.

10 ozs. of Young Fustic.

1 oz. of Dry Cochineal.

6 pints of Nitrate of Tin.

Boil 20 minutes.

No. 12.

15 *Pieces*, ¾ MOREENS.—BUFF.

Dry in a clean vessel with 3 ozs. of Dry Cochineal.

1½ lb. of Young Fustic.

6 lbs. of Tartar.

8 pints of Nitrate of Tin.

Darker shades may be dyed by adding more Cochineal, and the same quantity of other ingredients.

No. 13.

15 *Pieces*, ¾ MOREENS.—LIGHT GRAIN CRIMSON.

Dye in a clean vessel with 4 lbs. of Paste Cochineal.

2 lbs. of Dry Cochineal.

2 lbs. of Alum.

4 lbs. of Brown Tartar.

10 pints of Nitrate of Tin.

Boil 40 minutes.

No. 14.

15 *Pieces*, ¾ MOREENS.—DARK GRAIN · CRIMSON.

Dye in a clean vessel with 5 lbs. of Paste Cochineal.
2½ lbs. of Dry Cochineal.
5 lbs. of Brown Tartar.
3 lbs. of Alum.
6 quarts of Nitrate of Tin.
Boil 1 hour.

When the shades are not required very blue, more Dry Cochineal must be used, and less Paste Cochineal, and if wanted bluer, use more Paste Cochineal, and less Dry Cochineal.

———

No. 15.

15 *Pieces*, ¾ MOREENS.—COFFEE BROWN.

Dye with 30 lbs. of Camwood.
10 lbs. of Red Argol, or 20 lbs. of Super Argol.
1 pint of Chemic.
3 pints of Oil of Vitriol.
Boil 2 hours.

This shade of Color is not often wanted, but as it is sometimes called for, it is here inserted.

No. 16.

15 *Pieces*, ¾ MOREENS.—SEA GREEN.

Dye in a clean vessel, at boiling heat, with 5 lbs.
of Fustic.

1 tot of Liquid Extract.

20 lbs. of Alum.

7 lbs. of White Argol.

Boil 1 hour.

When the shade is required darker, add more Extract, and if Yellower, add more Fustic.

No. 17.

15 *Pieces*, ¾ MOREENS.—MOCK CRIMSON.

The Pieces must be boiled for 3 hours in a clean
vessel with 30 lbs. of Alum.

10 lbs. of White Argol or Brown Tartar.

1 quart of Nitrate of Tin.

After which, they must be well cleaned, and then
they must be finished in another clean vessel
with

25 lbs. of Peachwood.

3 gills of Nitrate of Tin.

5 pailfuls of Urine.

Boil a few Ends. Then clean and dry for the
press.

This color will very much approach the Grain
Crimson, but will not so well bear exposure to
the atmosphere.

No. 18.

15 *Pieces*, ¾ MOREENS.—BLACK.

Boil the pieces 40 minutes in a clean vessel with
2 lbs. of Red Argol.
1 lb. of Chrome.
Wash them and finish in another vessel with
20 lbs. of Logwood.
5 lbs. of Old Fustic.

Boil half an hour.

No. 19.

15 *Pieces*, ¾ MOREENS.—LIGHT SILVER DRAB.

Dye in a clean vessel with 10 lbs. of Super Argol.
1 quart of Oil of Vitriol.
1 handful of Paste Cudbear.
2 spoonfuls of Liquid Extract.

Boil 40 minutes.

No. 20.

15 *Pieces*, ¾ MOREENS.—FULL SILVER DRAB.

Dye in a clean vessel with 10 lbs. of Super Argol.
1 quart of Oil of Vitriol.
2 handfuls of Paste Cudbear.
1 handful of Madder.
4 spoonfuls of Liquid Extract.
Boil 1 hour.

If a darker shade is required, add more Liquid Extract to the other ingredients.

No. 21.

15 *Pieces*, ¾ MOREENS.—LIGHT FAWN.

Dye in a clean vessel with 10 lbs. of Super Argol.
1 quart of Oil of Vitriol.
2 handfuls of Madder.
The size of a Knor of Paste Cudbear.
1 spoonful of Liquid Extract.
Boil 1 hour.

17

No. 22.

14 *Pieces*, ¾ MOREENS.—DARKER FAWN.

Dye in a clean vessel with 10 lbs. of Super Argol.
1 quart of Oil of Vitriol.
2 spoonfuls of Liquid Extract.
4 handfuls of Madder.
1 handful of Paste Cudbear.
Boil to shade.

If a darker shade is required, add more Extract.

———

No. 23.

15 *Pieces*, ¾ MOREENS.—CINNAMON BROWN.

Dye in a clean vessel with 40 lbs. of Old Rasped
  Fustic.
2 lbs. of Camwood.
10 lbs. of Super Argol.
2 lbs. of Red Argol.
20 lbs. of Alum.
10 lbs. of Madder.

No. 24.

15 *Pieces*, ¾ MOREENS.—DARKER CINNAMON BROWN.

Dye with 50 lbs. of Old Rasped Fustic.

15 lbs. of Super Argol.

25 lbs. of Alum.

4 lbs. of Red Argol.

2½ lbs. of Camwood, or a handful of Cudbear may be used in the place of Camwood, which will produce the same effect.

Boil 1½ hour.

If a flatter shade is required, add a spoonful of Liquid Extract.

———

No. 25.

15 *Pieces*, ¾ MOREENS.—MIDDLE GREEN.

Dye in a clean vessel with 8 lbs. of White Argol.

15 lbs. of Alum.

1 gill of Chemic.

20 lbs. of Fustic.

Boil 1 hour.

No. 26.

15 *Pieces*, ¾ MOREENS.—DARK GREEN.

Dye with 8 lbs. of White Argol.

20 lbs. of Alum.

1 pint of Chemic.

25 lbs. of Fustic.

Boil 1 hour.

Darker shades of Green must have more Chemic, and if a Yellower shade is required, add more Fustic.

No. 27.

15 *Pieces*, ¾ MOREENS.—LIGHT GREEN.

Dye in a clean vessel with 15 lbs. of Alum.

8 lbs. of White Argol.

15 lbs. of Chipped Fustic.

1 tot of Liquid Extract.

Boil 1 hour.

No. 28.

15 *Pieces*, ¼ MOREENS.—DARKER GREEN.

Dye with 20 lbs. of Alum.

20 lbs. of Fustic.

8 lbs. of White Argol.

2 tots of Liquid Extract.

Boil 1 hour.

If the shade is required Bluer, add a little more Extract, and if Yellower, a little more Fustic.

No. 29.

15 *Pieces*, ¾ MOREENS.—LIGHT SAXON BLUE.

Dye in a clean vessel with 20 lbs. of Crystals.
2 quarts of Oil of Vitriol.
2 ozs. of Prussiate.
1 tot of Nitrate of Tin.
1 pint of Liquid Extract.

Boil 1 hour.

No. 30.

15 *Pieces*, ¾ MOREENS.—DARK SAXON BLUE.

Dye in a clean vessel with 20 lbs. of Crystals.
2 quarts of Oil of Vitriol.
4 ozs. of Prussiate.
1 tot of Nitrate of Tin.
3 gills of Liquid Extract.

Boil 1 hour.

If darker shades are required, add more Liquid Extract.

17*

No. 31.

15 *Pieces*, ¾ MOREENS.—LIGHT RED CRIMSON.

Dye in a clean vessel with 2 lbs. of Alum.
4 lbs. of Brown Tartar.
1½ lb. of Dry Cochineal.
4 quarts of Nitrate of Tin.
Boil 40 minutes.

No. 32.

15 *Pieces*, ¾ MOREENS.—FULL RED CRIMSON.

Dye in a clean vessel with 4 lbs. of Alum.
6 lbs. of Brown Tartar.
2½ lbs. of Dry Cochineal.
10 pints of Nitrate of Tin.
Boil 1 hour.

No. 33.

15 *Pieces*, ¾ MOREENS.—LIGHT ROSE COLOR.

Dye in a clean vessel with 1 lb. of Dry Cochineal.
4 lbs. of Brown Tartar.
2 lbs. of Alum.
6 pints of Nitrate of Tin.
Boil 40 minutes.

No. 34.

15 *Pieces*, ¾ MOREENS.—FULL ROSE COLOR.

Dye in a clean vessel with 1½ lb. of Dry Cochineal.

5 lbs. of Brown Tartar.

4 quarts of Nitrate of Tin.

2 lbs. of Alum.

Boil 1 hour.

If bluer shades are required, let one-half of the Cochineal be Paste, and the other half Dry, and rather less Spirits.

No. 35.

15 *Pieces*, ¾ MOREENS.—LIGHT SALMON.

Dye in a clean vessel with 4 ozs. of Dry Cochineal.

5 lbs. of Brown Tartar.

5 pints of Nitrate of Tin.

Boil 50 minutes.

No. 36.

15 *Pieces*, ¾ MOREENS.—FULL SALMON.

Dye in a clean vessel with 8 ozs. of Dry Cochineal.

10 pints of Nitrate of Tin.

6 lbs. of Tartar.

Boil 1 hour.

If a Yellower shade is required, add 4 ozs. of Ground Fustic.

No. 37.

15 *Pieces*, ¾ MOREENS.—LIGHT PINK.

Dye in a clean vessel with 10 ozs. of Paste Cochineal.

5 lbs. of Alum.

2 lbs. of White Tartar.

4 pints of Nitrate of Tin.

Boil 40 minutes.

No. 38.

15 *Pieces*, ¾ MOREENS.—FULL PINK.

Dye in a clean vessel with 1¼ lb. of Paste Cochineal.

4 lbs. of Alum.

4 lbs. of White Tartar.

6 pints of Nitrate of Tin.

Boil 1 hour.

Lighter or darker shades may be dyed by adding more or less Paste Cochineal with the same quantity of Acid.

TWO COLORED DAMASK-DYEING.

No. 1.

10 *Pieces*, ¾ COTTON AND WORSTED DA-MASKS.—SCARLET AND PINK.

In this color, the worsted must be first dyed Scarlet in a clean vessel with 12 lbs. of Lac Dye.

12 quarts of Nitrate of Tin.

10 lbs. of Young Fustic.

8 lbs. of White Argol or Brown Tartar.

Boil 1 hour.

The Pieces must then be well cleaned, and then Cotton dyed with Safflower. A light shade of Pink will take 1 lb. of Safflower to a Piece, and a dark shade 1½ lb. It must be spent according to Receipt 68, page 83. The clear Liquor must be put into a cistern of cold water, with about 1 pint of Oil of Vitriol, and 1 lb. of Tartaric Acid. The goods must then be entered and turned on in the Liquor until dyed to shade required.

If a Blue shade of Pink is required, rather less Oil of Vitriol must be used, and if a Redder shade, more must be used. Any shade of Pink may be dyed by adding more or less of the clear Safflower Liquor.

Various shades of Pink may be dyed from Peachwood, but none are equal to the Pink dyed with Safflower, when Scarlet and Pink are in the Piece together.

———

No. 2.

10 *Pieces*, ⁶⁄₄ COTTON AND WORSTED DAMASKS.—SCARLET AND YELLOW.

The Pieces in these two colors must be first dyed Scarlet, the same as in the last color, with the same quantity of ingredients, and then washed and Cotton dyed either through the Padding-Machine or in a cistern of cold or lukewarm water, with about 1 lb. of Turmeric to the Piece, more or less, according to shade of Yellow required.

The Turmeric must be boiled up with a little Oil of Vitriol; use about 1 lb. of Turmeric to 1 gallon of water, and take the clear Liquor only.

No. 3.

10 *Pieces*, $\frac{6}{4}$ COTTON AND WORSTED DAMASKS.—SCARLET AND FLESH COLOR.

Worsted Dye in Scarlet same as No. 1, and Cotton Dye either at the Padding-Machine, or in a clean vessel with 2 ozs. of Annotta, spent with 2 quarts of Water and 2 ozs. of Pearlash; boil well for a few minutes, so that every particle be dissolved. Take the clear Liquor.

A great variety of shades of cotton may be dyed by varying the quantity of Annotta, according to shade, using more for dark and less for light shades.

No. 4.

10 *Pieces*, $\frac{6}{4}$ COTTON AND WORSTED DAMASKS.—SCARLET AND SALMON.

First Worsted Dye in all respects for Scarlet same as No. 1, and Cotton Dye in a clean cistern of cold water with 5 lbs. of spent Safflower, and 1 lb. of Annotta spent with 1 lb. of Pearlash. Use the clear Liquor only. Give 10 Ends and wash off.

No. 5.

10 *Pieces*, DAMASKS.—SCARLET AND ROSE COLOR.

First Worsted Dye Scarlet same as No. 1, and Cotton Dye with 8 ozs. of Annotta spent with 8 ozs. of Pearlash, and the clear liquor from 6 lbs. of Safflower. Give 10 Ends, and wash off in another cistern of cold water with 1 pint of Oil of Vitriol in it. The Oil will raise both the Safflower and the Annotta.

This is, perhaps, one of the finest colors that can be dyed, more especially in a two colored Damask, possessing great brightness and beauty.

———

No. 6.

10 *Pieces*, $\frac{6}{4}$ DAMASKS.—LIGHT GREEN AND PINK.

First Worsted Dye Green in a clean vessel with
8 lbs. of White Argol.
20 lbs. of Fustic.
20 lbs. of Alum.
1 gill of Liquid Extract.
                    Boil 1 hour.

Clean and Cotton Dye in all respects the same as No. 1, with Safflower.

No. 7.

10 *Pieces*, ⁶⁄₄ COTTON AND WORSTED
DAMASKS.—MIDDLE GREEN
AND PINK.

First Worsted Dye with 20 lbs. of Fustic.
10 lbs. of Red Argol.
20 lbs. of Alum.
1 pint of Chemic.

Boil 1 hour.

If darker shades of Green are wanted, add
more Chemic according to shade.

Cotton Dye same as No. 1, with Safflower.

——

No. 8.

10 *Pieces*, ⁶⁄₄ COTTON AND WORSTED
DAMASKS.—GREEN AND
YELLOW.

This must be first Worsted Dyed according to
shade, and then washed and Cotton Dyed the
same as No. 2, with Turmeric.

——

No. 9.

10 *Pieces*, ⁶⁄₄ COTTON AND WORSTED
DAMASKS.—GREEN AND SALMON.

Worsted Dye to the shade of Green in the
same way as No. 7, using more or less Extract
18

according to shade required, and Cotton Dye in
all respects same as No. 4.

No. 10.

10 *Pieces*, ⁴⁄₄ COTTON AND WORSTED
DAMASKS.—SAXON BLUE AND
ROSE COLOR.

First Worsted Dye Saxon Blue in a clean vessel
 with
20 lbs. of Crystals.
2 quarts of Oil of Vitriol.
2 ozs. of Prussiate of Potash.
1 tot of Nitrate of Tin.
1 pint of Liquid Extract.
Wash and Cotton Dye in all respects the same as
 No. 5, with Safflower and Annotta.

A great variety of shades may be dyed in these
two colors by dyeing different shades of Blue and
varying the coloring of the Cotton as well.

No. 11.

10 *Pieces*, ⁴⁄₄ COTTON AND WORSTED
DAMASKS.—SKY BLUE AND PINK.

Worsted dye first in a clean vessel with
20 lbs. of Crystals.
3 pints of Oil of Vitriol.
2 ozs. of Prussiate.
2 spoonfuls of Nitrate of Tin.

Boil 40 minutes.

Wash and Cotton Dye with Safflower according to shade required, the same as No. 1.

———

No. 12.

10 *Pieces*, $\frac{6}{4}$ COTTON AND WORSTED DAMASK.—SKY BLUE AND PINK, ANOTHER WAY.

Worsted dye in all respects the same as No. 10.

And Cotton Dye by first sumaching the pieces with 2 lbs. of Sumach to the piece, run the pieces in the Sumach in the troughs 6 ends, then give 6 ends in Muriate of Tin, at 4° Twaddell, in another trough, then wash and dye with Peachwood Liquor according to shade, either in the troughs, or at the padding-machine, or in a cistern of cold water. A good full Pink will require about $1\frac{1}{2}$ lb. of Peachwood to a piece. Lighter or darker shades may be dyed by adding more or less Peachwood according to the shade.

———

No. 13.

10 *Pieces*, $\frac{6}{4}$ COTTON AND WORSTED DAMASKS.—BLUES AND CRIMSONS OF DIFFERENT SORTS.

Dye the worsted first a good Sky or Saxon Blue; or Royal Blue, if a very dark and bright blue is required, wash well and cotton dye same as No. 10, only use more Peachwood Liquor.

When a very full shade of Crimson is required, the Pieces should be sumached as before, and then passed through Nitrate of Iron, a few ends, in another trough or cistern; use about 2 quarts of Nitrate of Iron for the 10 Pieces. Then run in the Peachwood Liquor after running them 8 Ends, take up, and add 2 quarts of good Muriate of Tin to raise the Peachwood and brighten the color. By this mode, the fullest shades of Crimson may be dyed. It is the Nitrate of Iron that gives it the more fulness, and causes it to be darker with the same quantity of Peachwood.

No. 14.

10 *Pieces*, $\frac{6}{4}$ COTTON AND WORSTED DAMASKS.—GREEN AND CRIMSONS.

First dye Green, according to shade, same as No. 7, and Cotton Dye in all respects the same as No. 12.

The shade of color may be varied by dyeing the Worsted lighter or darker, and the same with respect to the Cotton.

It is impossible to give an estimate of the various shades produced by this variation.

No. 15.

10 *Pieces,* ⅘ COTTON AND WORSTED DA-
MASKS.—DARK BLUE AND ORANGE.

Worsted Dye first in a clean vessel with

1 quart of good Chemic.

20 lbs. of Crystals.

2 quarts of Oil of Vitriol.

Boil 1 hour, wash, and Cotton Dye by first
Sumaching the Pieces, and Spiriting them the
same as No. 11.

Then dye the Cotton with 3 lbs. of Peachwood,
and

2 lbs. of Quercitron Bark to the Piece.

This will very much imitate the Royal Blue
and Orange, but will not be so bright a color.

No. 16.

10 *Pieces,* ⅘ WORSTED AND COTTON
DAMASKS.—DARK BLUE
AND LIGHT ORANGE.

ANOTHER METHOD.

First Worsted Dye in a clean vessel with

20 lbs. of Crystals.

2 quarts of Oil of Vitriol.

1 quart of Chemic.

2 lbs. of Cudbear.

Wash well, and Cotton Dye with strong Annotta Liquor previously spent with Pearlash.

18*

The Annotta Orange will affect the Worsted more than the Peachwood Orange. It will tend to flatten it, and the reason that the Cudbear is given in Worsted Dyeing is that it may keep up the bloomy appearance.

Various shades may be dyed upon Cotton from Annotta, varying from a Light Straw color to a Full Orange; when the color is wanted very full, the Pieces should be passed through a weak decoction of Oil of Vitriol, after being run in the Annotta.

———

No. 17.

10 *Pieces*, ¾ COTTON AND WORSTED DAMASKS.—RUBY AND BLUE.

First Worsted Dye in a clean vessel with 10 lbs. of Cudbear. Boil 20 minutes.

Clean and Cotton Dye by running the Pieces in the Copperas Vat, one, two, or three ends, according to the shade of Blue required; then run the Pieces in a weak decoction of Oil of Vitriol, at about 100° Fahrenheit, to clear the Worsted and brighten the Cotton.

No. 18.

10 *Pieces*, $\frac{2}{4}$ COTTON AND WORSTED DAMASKS.—YELLOW AND BLUE.

First Cotton Dye in the Copperas Vat, clean
well, and then Worsted Dye in a clean vessel with
10 pints of Nitrate of Tin.
10 lbs. of Quercitron Bark.
6 lbs. of White Argol.
4 lbs. of Alum.

Boil 20 minutes.

No. 19.

10 *Pieces*, $\frac{2}{4}$ COTTON AND WORSTED DA-MASKS.—ORANGE AND BLUE.

Cotton dye Blue first, in the Copperas Vat, according to the shade required. Then wash, and
Worsted dye in a clean vessel with
6 lbs. of White Argol.
1½ lb. of Dry Cochineal.
10 lbs. of Young Fustic.
10 pints of Spirits.

Boil 40 minutes.

No. 20.

10 *Pieces*, 6/4 COTTON AND WORSTED DAMASKS.—SCARLET AND COMMON BLUE.

First Worsted dye a good Scarlet, same as No. 1, and Cotton dye by passing a few ends through the Copperas Vat, and then clear in a vessel of warm water with 1 gill of Oil of Vitriol in it.

This color is not so bright as the Scarlet and Royal Blue, or what is called Coffee and Blue.

I shall next insert two methods of dyeing Coffee and Royal Blue, for the information of those who have so often had these colors so uneven and dead, from a want of a proper method of dyeing them.

———

No. 21.

10 *Pieces*, 4/4 COTTON & WORSTED DAMASKS.—COFFEE & ROYAL BLUE.

The Worsted must be first dyed a good bright Scarlet, the same in every respect as No. 1. Then Cotton dye by passing through strong Nitrate of Iron in the troughs, at 4° Twaddell, and to which add 2 lbs. of Tin Crystals. In this turn 4 ends, and in another trough, with 2 quarts of Ammonia, pass through this out of the Iron, and repeat in each trough two or three times, until a Buff appearance is seen; then wash well. In another trough, or at the Padding-Machine, add 10 lbs. of Prussiate of Potash, previously dissolved; in this give 6 ends, and then add 1 pint of Oil of Vitriol, and give the Pieces 6 ends more. Wash off for the Drying-Machine.

Then you have a good full Royal Blue upon the Cotton. This will produce a good bright color, and if a lighter shade is required give less Prussiate.

Another mode of dyeing the Blue is by dyeing it after Buffing it, the same as dyeing Royal Blue with Blue Spirits and Prussiate. But the brightest is by first running the Pieces in Sumach, about 2 lbs. to the Piece, and a little Logwood with it, and then going through all the process, as stated in the first mode.

In this latter method, the Cotton gets a quantity of Logwood upon it which is risen to a sort of Claret when it enters the Nitrate of Iron and the Crystals of Tin, the Iron working up the darkness of the Logwood, and the Crystals of Tin producing the bloom. It is by this means that this is so much brighter and more bloomy than the other with the same quantity of Prussiate.

I think I have given as many shades in single and two colored Damasks as are generally dyed, and from these any dyer may, by varying the quantities, obtain a great variety more.

CAMLET-DYEING.

☞ THE FOLLOWING PIECES ARE ALL FOUR-QUARTERS.

No. 1.

10 *Pieces*, LONG CAMLETS.—SCARLET.

Dye at boiling heat in a clean vessel with 20 lbs. of Lac.

10 lbs. of Young Fustic.

15 lbs. of Brown or White Tartar.

15 quarts of Nitrate of Tin.

Boil 1½ hour, after which they must be well cleaned.

No. 2.

10 *Pieces*, LONG CAMLETS.—LIGHT ORANGE.

Dye at boiling heat in a clean vessel with

15 lbs. of Brown Tartar.

15 lbs. of Young Fustic.

15 quarts of Nitrate of Tin.

4 ozs. of Cochineal.

Boil 1 hour, after which, clean well and dry off.

No. 3.

10 *Pieces*, LONG CAMLETS.—FULL ORANGE.

Dye at boiling heat in a clean vessel with
15 lbs. of Young Fustic.
15 lbs. of Brown Tartar or White Argol.
1 lb. of Cochineal.
15 quarts of Nitrate of Tin.
    Boil 1 hour, after which, clean and dry off.

———

No. 4.

10 *Pieces*, CAMLETS.—LIGHT YELLOW.

Dye, at boiling heat, with 10 lbs. of Quercitron
  Bark.
10 quarts of Nitrate of Tin.
12 lbs. of Brown Tartar.
    Boil 1 hour, and then clean and dry off.

———

No. 5.

10 *Pieces*, CAMLETS.—FULL YELLOW.

Dye at boiling heat in a clean vessel with
20 lbs. of Young Fustic.
15 quarts of Nitrate of Tin.
15 lbs. of Brown Tartar.
    Boil 1 hour, and then clean and dry off.

No. 6.

10 *Pieces*, CAMLETS.—GRAIN CRIMSON.

Dye in a clean vessel with 5 lbs. of Paste Cochineal.

10 lbs. of Dry Cochineal.

15 lbs. of Brown Tartar.

15 quarts of Nitrate of Tin.

Boil 1 hour, and then wash off.

If fuller shades are wanted, add more Cochineal; if Bluer shades are required, add more Paste Cochineal: and the same quantity of other ingredients.

———

No. 7.

10 *Pieces*, CAMLETS.—ASH DRAB.

Dye at boiling heat in a clean vessel with

20 lbs. of Super Argol.

2 quarts of Sulphuric Acid.

1 lb. of Mull Madder.

1 lb. of Paste Cudbear.

¾ of a gill of Liquid Extract.

Boil 1 hour, and then clean and wash off.

Lighter or darker shades may be dyed by adding more or less Extract; when a Redder shade is required, add a little more Paste Cudbear.

No. 8.

10 *Pieces,* CAMLETS.—SILVER DRAB.

Dye in a clean vessel with 20 lbs. of Super Argol.

2 quarts of Sulphuric Acid.

½ lb. of Paste Cudbear.

1 tot of Liquid Extract.

Boil 1 hour, and then wash off.

———

No. 9.

10 *Pieces,* LONG CAMLETS.—FAWN DRAB.

Dye in a clean vessel with 20 lbs. of Super Argol.

2 quarts of Sulphuric Acid.

8 ozs. of Paste Cudbear.

6 spoonfuls of Liquid Extract.

2 lbs. of Mull Madder.

Boil 1 hour.

If darker shades are required, add more Liquid Extract.

19

No. 10.

10 *Pieces*, LONG CAMLETS.—SAXON BLUE.

Dye at boiling heat in a clean vessel with
20 lbs. of Crystals.
2 quarts of Sulphuric Acid.
3 gills of Liquid Extract.
4 ozs. of Prussiate of Potash.
1 tot of Nitrate of Tin.
      Boil 1 hour, and then clean and dry off.

———

No. 11.

10 *Pieces*, CAMLETS.—MAROON.

Dye in a clean vessel at boiling heat with
20 lbs. of Cudbear.
10 lbs. of Camwood.
1 gill of Sulphuric Acid.
      Boil 1 hour.

For fuller and Redder shades add more Camwood and a little more Sulphuric Acid.

This color might be dyed by first being boiled and finished in the same way as Mock Maroon, or Mock Crimson, but is not so permanent as by this Receipt.

No. 12.

10 *Pieces*, CAMLETS.—LIGHT BROWN.

Dye at boiling heat with 40 lbs. of Camwood.
1 pint of Chemic.
10 lbs. of Turmeric.
3 pints of Sulphuric Acid.
20 lbs. of Super Argol.

Boil 2 hours.

No. 13.

10 *Pieces*, CAMLETS.—DARK BROWN.

Dye with 60 lbs. of Camwood.
3 pints of Chemic.
20 lbs. of Super Argol.
3 pints of Sulphuric Acid.
10 lbs. of Turmeric.

Boil 2 hours.

Less Camwood will dye the same shade when the vessel is seasoned, by dyeing a similar color before it. Camwood requires to be well boiled to get the strength out of it, and also requires a strong Acid.

No. 14.

10 *Pieces*, CAMLETS.—CLARET BROWN.

First boil 40 minutes in a clean vessel with
2 lbs. of Chrome.
Then wash and finish in another vessel with
8 ozs. of Alum.
8 ozs. of Logwood.
20 lbs. Fustic.
30 lbs. of Peachwood.

Boil 1 hour in the finishing, then clean and dry off.

Lighter or darker shades may be dyed by adding or diminishing the quantity of Logwood, according to the shade required. A very small quantity of Logwood will make a great difference in the shade. By adding 1 oz. more to each Piece, it will be much darker.

The same shade of color may be dyed with Camwood, Chemic, and Acid, but it is more expensive, and sometimes the fabric is made tender by this process.

No. 15.

10 *Pieces*, LONG CAMLETS.—LIGHT PURPLE.

Boil 3 hours in a clean vessel with 50 lbs. of
  Alum.
10 lbs. of Red Argol.
10 lbs. of Logwood.
Wash well, and finish in a clean vessel with
10 lbs. of Cudbear.
5 quarts of Ammonia.

Clean and dry off.

No. 16.

10 *Pieces*, LONG CAMLETS.—MIDDLE PURPLE.

Boil 3 hours in a clean vessel with 50 lbs. of Alum.
10 lbs. of Argol.
20 lbs. of Logwood.
Clean well, and finish in a clean vessel with
10 lbs. of Cudbear.
6 quarts of Ammonia.

If a bluer shade of Purple is required, add
more Ammonia in the finishing, and when a Red
shade is required, add no Ammonia in the finishing.

19*

No. 17.

10 *Pieces*, LONG CAMLETS.—DARK PURPLE.

This color is dyed in all respects the same as the last, but must have more Logwood in the boiling, and a little more Ammonia in the finishing, in order to raise the Logwood.

No. 18.

10 *Pieces*, CAMLETS.—ANOTHER MODE OF DYEING PURPLES.

Boil 40 minutes with 2 lbs. of Chrome in a clean vessel; then wash well, and finish in another vessel of clean water with 10 lbs. of Cudbear and 10 lbs. of Logwood.

Clean and dry off.

Any shade of Purple may be dyed in this manner, using more Logwood for darker, and less for lighter shades.

No. 19.

10 *Pieces*, LONG CAMLETS.—BLUE BLACK.

Boil 40 minutes in a clean vessel with
2 lbs. of Chrome.
2 lbs. of Argol.
Finish in another vessel with 40 lbs. of Logwood.
Boil 40 minutes.

No. 20.

10 *Pieces*, LONG CAMLETS.—FULL BLACK.

Boil 40 minutes in a clean vessel with
2 lbs. of Chrome.
2 lbs. of Argol.
Finish in another vessel with
50 lbs. of Logwood.
10 lbs. of Fustic.

If not dark enough, add a few pounds more Logwood.

No. 21.

10 *Pieces*, LONG CAMLETS.—ROYAL BLUE.

In a clean vessel of water add
15 lbs. of Prussiate of Potash.
15 quarts of Royal Blue Spirits.

Heat up to 100°, enter the Pieces, and turn them half an hour; take them on to the wench, and heat the Liquor up to 140°, and put the Pieces into the Liquor again, and turn them half an hour more. Again take them to the wench, then heat the liquor up to 180°, and add 2 quarts of Finishing Spirits. Put the Pieces down again, and turn half an hour more. After which, take them out of the vessel, cool them over, heat the Liquor up to the boiling point, and add 3 quarts of Finishing Spirits; enter the Pieces again, boil half an hour, and then take out.

The Pieces will then be a good Light Royal Blue.

If a darker shade is required, add 2 quarts more Finishing Spirits, and 1, 2, or 3 lbs., or more or less, Logwood, according to the shade of darkness required; enter the Pieces again, and boil them half an hour more. Then take them out, cool them over, and clean off for the drying-machine.

The Logwood will produce a bloomy appearance, and make the color darker.

———

No. 22.

10 *Pieces*, LONG CAMLETS.—GREEN.

Dye in a clean vessel with 40 lbs. of Alum.
15 lbs. of White Argol.
40 lbs. of Chipped Fustic.
1 pint of Chemic.

Boil 1½ hour.

No. 23.

10 *Pieces*, LONG CAMLETS.—BOTTLE GREEN.

Dye in a clean vessel with 40 lbs. of Alum.
15 lbs. of White Argol.
50 lbs. of Old Fustic.
2 or 3 lbs. of Logwood.
3 quarts of Chemic.

Boil 1½ hour.

LASTING-DYEING.

—◆—

☞ THE FOLLOWING PIECES ARE ALL THREE-QUARTERS.

No. 1.

20 *Pieces*, LASTINGS.—LIGHT YELLOW.

Dye, at boiling heat, with 10 lbs. of Quercitron Bark.
10 quarts of Nitrate of Tin.
12 lbs. of Brown Tartar.
    Boil 1 hour, and then clean and dry off.

———

No. 2.

20 *Pieces*, LASTINGS.—FULL YELLOW.

Dye at boiling heat in a clean vessel with
20 lbs. of Young Fustic.
15 quarts of Nitrate of Tin.
15 lbs. of Brown Tartar.
    Boil 1 hour, and then clean and dry off.

No. 3.

20 *Pieces*, LASTINGS.—SILVER DRAB.

Dye in a clean vessel with 20 lbs. of Super Argol.
2 quarts of Sulphuric Acid.
½ lb. of Paste Cudbear.
1 tot of Liquid Extract.
> Boil 1 hour, and then wash off.

———

No. 4.

20 *Pieces*, LASTINGS.—ASH DRAB.

Dye at boiling heat in a clean vessel with
20 lbs. of Super Argol.
2 quarts of Sulphuric Acid.
1 lb. of Mull Madder.
1 lb. of Paste Cudbear.
¾ of a gill of Liquid Extract.
> Boil 1 hour, and then clean and wash off.

Lighter or darker shades may be dyed by adding more or less Extract; when a Redder shade is required, add a little more Paste Cudbear.

No. 5.

20 *Pieces*, LASTINGS.—FAWN DRAB.

Dye in a clean vessel with 20 lbs. of Super Argol.

2 quarts of Sulphuric Acid.

8 ozs. of Paste Cudbear.

6 spoonfuls of Liquid Extract.

2 lbs. of Mull Madder.

Boil 1 hour.

If darker shades are required, add more Liquid Extract.

———

No. 6.

20 *Pieces*, LASTINGS.—SAXON BLUE.

Dye at boiling heat in a clean vessel with

20 lbs. of Crystals.

2 quarts of Sulphuric Acid.

3 gills of Liquid Extract.

4 ozs. of Prussiate of Potash.

1 tot of Nitrate of Tin.

Boil one hour, and then clean and dry off.

No. 7.

20 *Pieces*, LASTINGS.—GRAIN CRIMSON.

Dye in a clean vessel with 5 lbs. of Paste Cochineal.

10 lbs. of Dry Cochineal.

15 lbs. of Brown Tartar.

15 quarts of Nitrate of Tin.

Boil 1 hour, and then wash off.

If fuller shades are wanted, add more Cochineal; if Bluer shades are required, add more Paste Cochineal: and the same quantity of other ingredients.

———

No. 8.

20 *Pieces*, LASTINGS.—SCARLET.

Dye at boiling heat in a clean vessel with 20 lbs. of Lac.

10 lbs. of Young Fustic.

15 lbs. of Brown or White Tartar.

15 quarts of Nitrate of Tin.

Boil 1½ hour, after which they must be well cleaned.

20

No. 9.

20 *Pieces*, LASTINGS.—LIGHT ORANGE.

Dye at boiling heat in a clean vessel with

15 lbs. of Brown Tartar.

15 lbs. of Young Fustic.

15 quarts of Nitrate of Tin.

4 ozs. of Cochineal.

Boil 1 hour, after which clean well and dry off.

———

No. 10.

20 *Pieces*, LASTINGS.—FULL ORANGE.

Dye at boiling heat in a clean vessel with

15 lbs. of Young Fustic.

15 lbs. of Brown Tartar or White Argol.

1 lb. of Cochineal.

15 quarts of Nitrate of Tin.

Boil 1 hour, after which clean and dry off.

———

No. 11.

20 *Pieces*, LASTINGS.—MAROON.

Dye in a clean vessel at boiling heat with

20 lbs. of Cudbear.

10 lbs. of Camwood.

1 gill of Sulphuric Acid.

Boil 1 hour.

For fuller and Redder shades add more Camwood and a little more Sulphuric Acid.

This color might be dyed by first being boiled

and finished in the same way as Mock Maroon, or Mock Crimson, but is not so permanent as by this Receipt.

***

No. 12.

20 *Pieces*, LASTINGS.—LIGHT BROWN.

Dye at boiling heat with 40 lbs. of Camwood.
1 pint of Chemic.
10 lbs. of Turmeric.
3 pints of Sulphuric Acid.
20 lbs. of Super Argol.

Boil 2 hours.

***

No. 13.

20 *Pieces*, LASTINGS.—GREEN.

Dye in a clean vessel with 40 lbs. of Alum.
15 lbs. of White Argol.
40 lbs. of Chipped Fustic.
1 pint of Chemic.

Boil 1½ hour.

***

No. 14.

20 *Pieces*, LASTINGS.—BOTTLE GREEN.

Dye in a clean vessel with 40 lbs. of Alum.
15 lbs. of White Argol.
50 lbs. of Old Fustic.
2 or 3 lbs. of Logwood.
3 quarts of Chemic.

Boil 1½ hour.

No. 15.

20 *Pieces*, LASTINGS.—BLUE BLACK.

Boil 40 minutes in a clean vessel with

2 lbs. of Chrome.

2 lbs. of Argol.

Finish in another vessel with 40 lbs. of Logwood.
Boil 40 minutes.

No. 16.

20 *Pieces*, LASTINGS.—FULL BLACK.

Boil 40 minutes in a clean vessel with

2 lbs. of Chrome.

2 lbs. of Argol.

Finish in another vessel with

50 lbs. of Logwood.

10 lbs. of Fustic.

If not dark enough, add a few pounds more Logwood.

No. 17.

20 *Pieces*, LASTINGS.—CLARET BROWN.

First boil 40 minutes in a clean vessel with

2 lbs. of Chrome.

Then wash and finish in another vessel with

8 ozs. of Alum.

8 ozs. of Logwood.

20 lbs. of Fustic.

30 lbs. of Peachwood.

Boil 1 hour in the finishing, then clean and dry off.

Lighter or darker shades may be dyed by adding or diminishing the quantity of Logwood, according to the shade required. A very small quantity of Logwood will make a great difference in the shade. By adding 1 oz. more to each Piece, it will be much darker.

The same shade of color may be dyed with Camwood, Chemic, and Acid, but it is more expensive, and sometimes the fabric is made tender by this process.

No. 18.

20 *Pieces*, LASTINGS.—DARK BROWN.

Dye with 60 lbs. of Camwood.
3 pints of Chemic.
20 lbs. of Super Argol.
3 pints of Sulphuric Acid.
10 lbs. of Turmeric.

Boil 2 hours.

Less Camwood will dye the same shade when the vessel is seasoned, by dyeing a similar color before it. Camwood requires to be well boiled to get the strength out of it, and also requires a strong Acid.

No. 19.

20 *Pieces*, LASTINGS.—LIGHT PURPLE.

Boil 3 hours in a clean vessel with 50 lbs. of Alum.
10 lbs. of Red Argol.
10 lbs. of Logwood.
Wash well, and finish in a clean vessel with
10 lbs. of Cudbear.
5 quarts of Ammonia.
Clean and dry off.

———

No. 20.

20 *Pieces*, LASTINGS.—MIDDLE PURPLE.

Boil 3 hours in a clean vessel with 50 lbs. of Alum.
10 lbs. of Argol.
20 lbs. of Logwood.
Clean well, and finish in a clean vessel with
10 lbs. of Cudbear.
6 quarts of Ammonia.

If a Bluer shade of Purple is required, add more ammonia in the finishing, and when a Red shade is required, add no Ammonia in the finishing.

No. 21.

20 *Pieces*, LASTINGS.—DARK PURPLE.

This color is dyed in all respects the same as the last, but must have more Logwood in the boiling, and a little more Ammonia in the finishing, in order to raise the Logwood.

No. 22.

20 *Pieces*, LASTINGS.—ROYAL BLUE.

In a clean vessel of water add
15 lbs. of Prussiate of Potash.
15 quarts of Royal Blue Spirits.

Heat up to 100°, enter the pieces, and turn them half an hour; take them on to the wench, and heat the Liquor up to 140°, and put the Pieces into the Liquor again, and turn them half an hour more. Again take them on to the wench, then heat the Liquor up to 180°, and add 2 quarts of Finishing Spirits. Put the Pieces down again, and turn half an hour more. After which, take them out of the vessel, cool them over, heat the Liquor up to the boiling point, and add 3 quarts of Finishing Spirits; enter the Pieces again, boil half an hour, and then take out.

The Pieces will then be a good Light Royal Blue.

If a darker shade is required, add 2 quarts more Finishing Spirits, and 1, 2, or 3 lbs., or more or less, Logwood, according to the shade of darkness required; enter the Pieces again, and boil them half an hour more. Then take them out, cool them over, and clean off for the drying-machine.

The Logwood will produce a bloomy appearance, and make the color darker.

———

No. 23.

20 *Pieces*, LASTINGS.—ANOTHER MODE OF DYEING PURPLES.

Boil 40 minutes with 2 lbs. of Chrome in a clean vessel, then wash well, and finish in another vessel of clean water with 10 lbs. of Cudbear and 10 lbs. of Logwood. Clean and dry off.

Any shade of purple may be dyed in this manner, using more Logwood for darker, and less for lighter shades.

SHOT COBOURG DYEING.

☞ ORLEANS ARE DYED IN THE SAME WAY AS COBOURGS.

No. 1.

10 *Pieces*, ⁶⁄₄ SHOT COBOURGS.—BLUE AND PINK.

Worsted Dye with 2 tots of Liquid Extract.

3 pints of Oil of Vitriol.

10 lbs. of Crystals.

Clean and Cotton Dye with 1 pint of Spent or Bottled Safflower.

1 tot of Oil of Vitriol.

Then wash off.

No. 2.

10 *Pieces*, ⁶⁄₄ SHOT COBOURGS.—YELLOW AND BLUE.

Worsted Dye in a clean vessel with 2 lbs. of White Argol.

5 pints of Nitrate of Tin.

7½ lbs. of Young Fustic.

Clean and Cotton Dye by first running them 20 minutes through Nitrate of Iron Liquor, 3 gills to a Piece, then through 1½ lb. of melted Prussiate of Potash in a separate Vessel, 6 ends; then take up and add 1 gill of Oil of Vitriol, run 8 ends, and then clean off.

———

No. 3.

10 *Pieces*, ¾ SHOT COBOURGS.—ORANGE AND BLUE.

Worsted Dye with 2 lbs. of Argol.
5 pints of Nitrate of Tin.
10 lbs. of Young Fustic.
1½ lbs. of Cochineal.
                Cotton Dye same as No. 2.

———

No. 4.

10 *Pieces*, ¾ SHOT COBOURGS.—CRIMSON AND BLUE.

Worsted Dye with 3 lbs. of Argol.
5 pints of Nitrate of Tin.
5 lbs. of Cochineal.
                Cotton Dye same as No. 2.

No. 5.

10 *Pieces,* ¾ SHOT COBOURGS.—RUBY AND BLUE.

Worsted Dye with 6 lbs. of Cudbear.
Cotton Dye same as No. 2.
Darker shades of Blue may be got by adding more Prussiate.

No. 6.

10 *Pieces,* ¾ SHOT COBOURGS.— LAVENDER AND PINK.

Worsted Dye with 2 tots of Liquid Extract.
1 lb. of Paste Cudbear.
3 pints of Oil of Vitriol.
10 lbs. of Crystals.

Cotton Dye by first running them through 20 lbs. of Sumach, 8 ends, then through 2 quarts of Nitrate of Iron; clean, and run them through 2 Pailfuls of strong Peachwood Liquor, then through 3 pints of Orleans Spirits, and clean off.

No. 7.

10 *Pieces,* ⁶⁄₄ SHOT COBOURGS.—GREEN AND PINK.

Worsted Dye with 2 tots of Liquid Extract.
20 lbs. of Old Fustic.
10 lbs. of Alum.
2 lbs. of Argol.
      Cotton Dye same as No. 6, or No. 1.

No. 8.

10 *Pieces,* ⁶⁄₄ SHOT COBOURGS.— LAVENDER AND CRIMSON.

Worsted Dye with 2½ tots of Liquid Extract.
3 pints of Oil of Vitriol.
10 lbs. of Crystals.
    To Cotton Dye them, Sumach and Spiritth em, then run through Peachwood Liquor, and Spirit again.

No. 9.

10 *Pieces,* ⁶⁄₄ SHOT COBOURGS.—DARK SKY AND CRIMSON.

    Worsted Dye as No. 8, but add 2 tots more of Liquid Extract.
    Cotton Dye same as No. 8, but with stronger Peachwood Liquor.

No. 10.

10 *Pieces*, $\frac{5}{4}$ SHOT COBOURGS.—LIGHT GREEN AND SALMON.

Worsted Dye with 1 tot of Liquid Extract.
10 lbs. of Alum.
2 lbs. of Argol.
20 lbs. of Old Fustic.

Cotton Dye same as No. 8, but with less Peach-wood Liquor.

No. 11.

10 *Pieces*, $\frac{6}{4}$ SHOT COBOURGS.—GREEN AND PINK.

Worsted Dye with 3 tots of Liquid Extract.
10 lbs. of Alum.
2 lbs. of Argol.
30 lbs. of Fustic.

Cotton Dye same as No. 6.

No. 12.

10 *Pieces*, SHOT COBOURGS.—GREEN AND CLARET.

Worsted Dye with 1 pint of Chemic.
10 lbs. of Alum.
2 lbs. of Argol.
20 lbs. of Fustic.

Cotton Dye by running them in Sumach, then

21

in Iron Liquor, and then in Spirits, 8 ends in each; clean and run them in a cistern of cold water, with 10 lbs. of spent Logwood, and clean them.

No. 13.

10 *Pieces*, ⅞ SHOT COBOURGS.—GREEN AND PURPLE.

Worsted Dye with 1 gill of Chemic.
20 lbs. of Old Fustic.
10 lbs. of Alum.
2 lbs. of Argol.

Cotton Dye by running them in Sumach, then through 1 quart of Muriate of Tin, then in a cistern of cold water, with 10 lbs. of spent Logwood; after running them 8 ends, take up and add 10 ozs. of Crystals of Tin, and run 8 ends more.

No. 14.

10 *Pieces*, ⅞ SHOT COBOURGS.—BLACK AND CRIMSON.

Worsted Dye Black in the following manner: Boil 20 minutes with 2 lbs. of Chrome, then run them through Sumach and Iron separately; clean, and finish with 50 lbs. of Logwood, 15 lbs. of Fustic, 2 lbs. of Red Argol, and boil them half an hour. Similar shades may be got, but not equally approved, being dearer, by being Sumached and Ironed first, and then Chromed. The Cotton may be dyed after the Worsted is dyed Black, by being Sumached, Ironed, and filled up with Logwood, which for coarse rough Goods is perhaps preferable.

Cotton Dye by running them in Sumach and Iron, then clean; boil up 20 lbs. of Peachwood in the bottom of a cistern, run 8 ends, then take up and add 3 quarts of Muriate of Tin, and run other 8 ends.

———

No. 15.

10 *Pieces*, ¾ SHOT COBOURGS.—LIGHT OLIVE AND CRIMSON.

Worsted Dye with 5 spoonfuls of Liquid Extract.
10 lbs. of Alum.
2 lbs. of Argol.
20 lbs. of Fustic.
Cotton Dye same as No. 14.

———

No. 16.

10 *Pieces*, SHOT COBOURGS.—ORANGE AND PURPLE.

Worsted Dye with 2 lbs. of White Argol.
5 pints of Nitrate of Tin.
1¼ lbs. of Cochineal.
7½ lbs. of Young Fustic.
Cotton Dye same as No. 13.

No. 17.

10 *Pieces*, ⁹⁄₄ SHOT COBOURGS.—ROYAL BLUE AND FULL PINK.

Worsted Dye with 5 lbs. of Prussiate.

10 pints of Blue Spirits.

5 pints of Finishing Spirits.

Heat up, according to No. 22 of Lastings.

Cotton Dye by running them through Sumach, Iron, and Spirits, separately; then through 20 lbs. of Spent Peachwood, and clean them.

No. 18.

10 *Pieces*, ⁹⁄₄ SHOT COBOURGS.—GREEN AND ORANGE.

Worsted Dye with 20 lbs. of Fustic.

3 gills of Chemic.

10 lbs. of Alum.

2 lbs. of Argol; clean, and

Cotton Dye by running them in Sumach and Spirits separately, and then boil up in the bottom of a cistern.

10 lbs. of Peachwood.

10 lbs. of Quercitron Bark.

2 lbs. of Alum.

Run them 10 ends.

Lighter or Darker shades of Orange may be got by adding more or less Peachwood.

SILK STRIPED ORLEANS,

FROM BLACK, WHITE, AND COLORED WARPS.

———•———

No. 1.

6 *Pieces*, ⅜ SILK STRIPES.—LIGHT OLIVE FROM BLACK WARP.

Dye with 6 lbs. of Turmeric.
4 lbs. of Logwood.
1 lb. of Blue Vitriol.
> Boil 40 minutes, and clean off.

———

No. 2.

6 *Pieces*, ⅜ SILK STRIPES.—DARK OLIVE FROM BLACK WARP.

Boil 20 minutes with 12 ozs. of Chrome.
Clean, and finish in a clean vessel with 4 lbs. of Turmeric.
1½ lb. of Logwood.
> Boil 30 minutes, and clean off.

21*

No. 3.

6 *Pieces*, ⁹⁄₄ SILK STRIPES.—BROWN OLIVE FROM BLACK WARP.

Dye with 6 lbs. of Turmeric.
4 lbs. of Peachwood.
6 lbs. of Logwood.
½ lb. of Alum.
1 lb. of Blue Vitriol.   Boil 40 minutes.

No. 4.

6 *Pieces*, ⁹⁄₄ SILK STRIPES.—RED BROWN FROM PURPLE WARP.

Dye with 12 lbs. of Peachwood.
2 lbs. of Alum.
1 lb. of Logwood.
2 lbs. of Turmeric.   Boil 40 minutes.

No. 5.

6 *Pieces*, ⁹⁄₄ SILK STRIPES.—DARK CLARET FROM BLACK WARP.

Chrome same as No. 2.
Finish with 2 lbs. of Cudbear.
6 lbs. of Peachwood.
2 lbs. of Logwood.
12 ozs. of Alum.

Boil half an hour.

No. 6.

6 *Pieces,* ¾ SILK STRIPES.—CHROMED BROWN, PURPLE WARP.

Chrome same as No. 2.
Finish with 2 lbs. of Logwood.
12 lbs. of Peachwood.
12 ozs. of Alum.

Boil half an hour.

No. 7.

6 *Pieces,* ¾ SILK STRIPES.—CLARET BROWN FROM CLARET WARP.

Dye with 12 lbs. of Peachwood.
2 lbs. of Alum.

Boil half an hour.

No. 8.

6 *Pieces,* ¾ SILK STRIPES.—DARK CLARET BROWN FROM CLARET WARP.

Dye with 12 lbs. of Peachwood.
4 lbs. of Logwood.
1 lb. of Alum.
1 lb. of Blue Vitriol.

Boil half an hour.

No. 9.

6 *Pieces*, $\frac{6}{4}$ SILK STRIPES.—CHROMED CLARET FROM CLARET PURPLE WARP.

Chrome same as No. 2.
Finish with 12 lbs. of Peachwood.
2 lbs. of Cudbear.

Boil half an hour.

———

No. 10.

6 *Pieces*, $\frac{6}{4}$ SILK STRIPES.—DARK CLARET FROM PURPLE WARP.

Chrome same as No. 2.
Finish with 12 lbs. of Peachwood.
1 lb. of Cudbear.
1 lb. of Logwood.

Boil half an hour.

———

No. 11.

6 *Pieces*, $\frac{6}{4}$ SILK STRIPES.—RUBY FROM VIOLET WARP.

Dye with 6 lbs. of Cudbear.

Boil 20 minutes.

No. 12.

6 *Pieces*, ¾ SILK STRIPES.—LIGHT CLARET FROM PURPLE WARP.

Boil 1 hour with 6 lbs. of Alum.
12 ozs. of Logwood.
Clean and finish with 12 lbs. of Peachwood.
1 lb. of Cudbear.
Boil 20 minutes.

No. 13.

6 *Pieces*, ¾ SILK STRIPES.—DARKER CLARET FROM CLARET WARP.

Boil 1 hour with 6 lbs. of Alum.
3 lbs. of Logwood.
Clean and finish with 12 lbs. of Peachwood.
1 lb. of Cudbear.
1 quart of Ammonia.
Boil 20 minutes.

No. 14.

6 *Pieces*, ¾ SILK STRIPES.—ADELAIDE FROM BLACK WARP.

Chrome same as No. 2.
Finish with 3 lbs. of Cudbear.
2 lbs. of Logwood.
Boil half an hour.

No. 15.

6 *Pieces*, ⁶⁄₄ SILK STRIPES.—DARK MUL-
    BERRY FROM BLACK WARP.

Chrome as No. 2.
Finish with 4 lbs. of Logwood.
3 lbs. of Cudbear.
1 quart of Ammonia.
> Boil half an hour.

——

No. 16.

6 *Pieces*, ⁶⁄₄ SILK STRIPES.—ADELAIDE
    FROM BLACK WARP.

Chrome as No. 2.
Finish with 2½ lbs. of Logwood.
2 lbs. of Cudbear.
1 pint of Ammonia.
> Boil half an hour.

——

No. 17.

6 *Pieces*, ⁶⁄₄ SILK STRIPES.—VIOLET
    FROM VIOLET WARP.

Run 2 ends through the Copperas Vat.
Finish with 4 lbs. of Cudbear.
> Boil half an hour.

No. 18.

6 *Pieces*, ¾ SILK STRIPES.—ROYAL BLUE FROM WHITE WARP.

First prepare the Cotton by running them 18 ends
in 3 gallons of Nitrate of Iron, then clean and
Worsted Dye with 4½ lbs. of Prussiate.

4 quarts of Blue Spirits.

2 quarts of Finishing Spirits.

Heat up to 100°.

When a Buffing Machine is used, much less Iron
will do.

———

No. 19.

6 *Pieces*, SILK STRIPES.—LAVENDER FROM WHITE WARP.

First run 1 end in the Copperas Vat, then Worsted
Dye in a clean vessel with 1 lb. of White Argol.

2 lbs. of Alum.

6 spoonfuls of Liquid Extract.

1 handful of Cudbear.

Redden in a cistern of Cold Water with 2 quarts
of Red Liquor, and 1 lb. of spent Logwood.

No. 20.

6 *Pieces*, ¾ SILK STRIPES.—RED BROWN FROM PURPLE WARP.

Chrome as No. 2.
Finish with 6 lbs. of Peachwood.
6 lbs. of Turmeric.
1 lb. of Alum.
Boil half an hour.

No. 21.

5 *Pieces*, SILK STRIPES.—GREEN FROM WHITE WARP.

Worsted Dye with 1 gill of Chemic.
12 lbs. of Fustic.
6 lbs. of Alum.
1 lb. of Argol.

Clean and Silk Dye with a little Sweet Extract,
at 80°, then Cotton Dye by running them
through Sumach and Iron separately, then clean
again, and run through 3 lbs. of Spent Logwood
in Cold Water.

No. 22.

6 *Pieces*, ⅔ SILK STRIPES.—SOLID GRAIN PINK FROM WHITE WARP.

Worsted Dye with 5 pints of Nitrate of Tin.

2 lbs. of White Argol.

5 ozs. of Dry Cochineal.

5 ozs. of Paste Cochineal.

Clean and Cotton Dye with 1 pint of spent or bottled Safflower, and 1 tot of Oil of Vitriol, in a cistern of clean water.

ANOTHER MODE.

Cotton and Silk Dye together by running them in a little Red Liquor, and then through a little Cochineal previously scalded and settled, and use only the clear Liquor.

In this instance, the Cotton, Silk, and Worsted are all dyed from Cochineal, a thing I never saw or knew before I tried it.

22

COLORED ORLEANS,

FROM BLACK WARPS.

No. 1.

10 *Pieces*, ⁶⁄₄ ORLEANS.—LIGHT BROWN.

First run 8 ends in 1 quart of Orleans Spirits.
Clean and then dye with 10 lbs. of Turmeric.
10 lbs. of Peachwood.
2 lbs. of Logwood.
2½ lbs. of Blue Vitriol.
1 lb. of Alum.

Boil 40 minutes.

No. 2.

10 *Pieces*, ⁶⁄₄ ORLEANS.—CHROMED BROWN.

Boil 20 minutes with 1 lb. of Chrome.
Clean and finish with 20 lbs. of Peachwood.
5 lbs. of Turmeric.
½ lb. of Alum.

Boil half an hour.

No. 3.

10 *Pieces*, ⅜ ORLEANS.—CLARET.

Spirit same as No. 1.
Boil 1 hour with 10 lbs. of Alum.
2 lbs. of Logwood.
Clean and finish with 20 lbs. of Peachwood.
2 quarts of Ammonia.
> Boil half an hour in the finishing.

——

No. 4.

10 *Pieces*, ⅜ ORLEANS.—DARK CLARET.

Spirit same as No. 1.
Boil 1 hour with 10 lbs. of Alum.
8 lbs. of Logwood.
Clean and finish with 12 lbs. of Peachwood.
3 quarts of Ammonia.
> Boil half an hour in the finishing.

——

No. 5.

10 *Pieces*, ⅜ ORLEANS.—BLUE CLARET.

Chrome same as No. 2.
Finish with 2 lbs. of Cudbear.
10 lbs. of Peachwood.
> Boil half an hour.

No. 6.

10 *Pieces*, ⁶⁄₄ ORLEANS.—VIOLET.

Dye with 8 lbs. of Cudbear.
Run them 2 ends through the Copperas Vat.
Boil half an hour.

———

No. 7.

10 *Pieces*, ⁶⁄₄ ORLEANS.—ADELAIDE.

Chrome same as No. 2.
Finish with 4 lbs. of Cudbear.
6 lbs. of Peachwood.
2 lbs. of Logwood.
Boil half an hour.

———

No. 8.

10 *Pieces*, ⁶⁄₄ ORLEANS.—DARK CLARET BROWN.

Chrome same as No. 2.
Finish with 20 lbs. of Peachwood.
1 lb. of Logwood.
2 ozs. of Alum.
Boil half an hour.

No. 9.

10 *Pieces*, ⁴⁄₄ ORLEANS.—DARK BROWN OLIVE.

Chrome same as No. 2.
Finish with 10 lbs. of Turmeric.
10 lbs. of Peachwood.
2 lbs. of Logwood.
Boil half an hour.

———

No. 10.

10 *Pieces*, ⁴⁄₄ ORLEANS.—GREEN OLIVE.

Chrome same as No. 2.
Finish with 20 lbs. of Fustic.
4 lbs. of Logwood.
2 ozs. of Alum.
Boil 40 minutes.

———

No. 11.

10 *Pieces*, ⁴⁄₄ ORLEANS.—DARKER GREEN OLIVE.

Chrome same as No. 2.
Finish with 5 lbs. of Logwood.
8 lbs. of Turmeric.
4 ozs. of Alum.
Boil half an hour.
22*

No. 12.

10 *Pieces*, ⁴⁄₄ ORLEANS.—CHROMED GREEN.

Chrome same as No. 2.
Finish with 10 lbs. of Fustic.
5 lbs. of Logwood.

Boil half an hour.

———

No. 13.

10 *Pieces*, ⁴⁄₄ ORLEANS.—INVISIBLE GREEN.

Chrome same as No. 2, Silk Stripes.
Finish with 15 lbs. of Logwood.
10 lbs. of Fustic.

Boil half an hour.

Lighter or Darker shades may be obtained by using more or less Logwood.

———

No. 14.

10 *Pieces*, ⁴⁄₄ ORLEANS.—BLUE BLACK.

Boil 20 minutes with 1 lb. of Chrome.
Finish with 20 lbs. of Logwood.

Boil half an hour.

No. 15.

10 *Pieces*, ¾ ORLEANS.—FULL BLACK.

Chrome same as No. 14.

Finish with 25 lbs. of Logwood.

10 lbs. of Fustic.

1 lb. of Red Argol.

Boil half an hour.

COLORED
ORLEANS AND COBOURGS,

FROM WHITE WARPS.

No. 1.

10 *Pieces*, $\frac{6}{4}$ CINNAMON BROWN.

Run 8 Ends in 20 lbs. of Sumach.

Then 8 Ends in 2 Quarts of Nitrate of Iron.

1 Pint of Muriate of Tin.

Each in a separate vessel; then clean them, and dye off with 15 lbs. of Turmeric.

2 lbs. of Peachwood.

2½ lbs. of Alum, and

2½ lbs. of Blue Vitriol.

Boil half an hour, and clean off.

No. 2.

10 *Pieces*, $\frac{6}{4}$ RED BROWN.

Prepare as No. 1, Dye with 20 lbs. of Peachwood.

2 lbs. of Logwood.

5 lbs. Turmeric.

2½ lbs. of Alum, and

2½ lbs. of Blue Vitriol.

No. 3.

10 *Pieces*, ⅘ COFFEE BROWN.

Prepare as No. 1, Dye with 25 lbs. of Peachwood.
15 lbs. of Logwood.
8 lbs. of Turmeric.
2½ lbs. of Alum, and
2½ lbs. of Blue Vitriol.

—

No. 4.

10 *Pieces*, ⅘ LIGHT CLARET.

Run them 8 Ends in 20 lbs. of Sumach.
Then in 2 Quarts of Nitrate of Iron.
8 Ends in 1 Quart of Muriate of Tin.
Each in a separate vessel.

Clean and run them through 10 lbs. of Logwood, in a cistern of cold water, then boil them 1
hour with 10 lbs. of Alum, clean and finish with
20 lbs. of Peachwood, and 2 Quarts of Ammonia;
boil 20 minutes in finishing.

No. 5.

10 *Pieces*, ⅔ MIDDLE CLARET.

Prepare same as No. 4.

Boil 1 hour with 10 lbs. of Alum.

5 lbs. of Logwood.

Clean and finish with 20 lbs. of Peachwood.

2 quarts of Ammonia.

No. 6.

10 *Pieces*, ⅔ DARK CLARET.

Prepare same as No. 4.

Boil 1 hour with 10 lbs. of Logwood.

10 lbs. of Alum.

Clean and finish with 20 lbs. of Peachwood.

3 quarts of Ammonia.

No. 7.

10 *Pieces*, ⅔ CHROMED CLARET.

Prepare same as No. 4.

Clean and boil 20 minutes with 1 lb. of Chrome.

Finish in another vessel with 15 lbs. of Peachwood.

2 lbs. of Logwood.

¼ lb. of Alum.

No. 8.

10 *Pieces*, ⁶⁄₄ ADELAIDE.

Prepare same as No. 4.

Chrome same as No. 7.

Finish with 5 lbs. of Cudbear.

2 lbs. of Logwood.

Boil half an hour.

No. 9.

10 *Pieces*, ⁶⁄₄ MULBERRY.

Prepare same as No. 4.

Chrome same as No. 7.

Finish with 5 lbs. of Cudbear.

2 lbs. of Logwood.

Boil half an hour.

No. 10.

10 *Pieces*, ⁶⁄₄ APPLE GREEN.

Worsted Dye with 5 lbs. of Turmeric.

$\frac{1}{2}$ gill of Chemic.

10 lbs. of Super Argol.

1 quart of Oil of Vitriol.

Clean and run them 8 ends in 20 lbs. of Sumach.

8 ends in 2 quarts of Nitrate of Iron.

Clean again, then dye off with 6 lbs. of Turmeric.

1 lb. of Blue Vitriol, and clean off.

No. 11.

10 *Pieces*, ⅔ LIGHT OLIVE.

Worsted Dye with 1 gill of Chemic.

5 lbs. of Turmeric.

10 lbs. of Super Argol.

1 quart of Oil of Vitriol.

       In other respects, same as No. 10.

Olives of this and darker shades may be got from Chroming, but not to appear so Green when looked through the Piece.

———

No. 12.

10 *Pieces*, ⅔ DARK GREEN OLIVE.

Worsted Dye with 3 gills of Chemic.

5 lbs. of Turmeric.

10 lbs. of Super Argol.

1 quart of Oil of Vitriol.

Clean, then Sumach and Iron, and clean again, then

Dye them off with 5 lbs. of Logwood.

5 lbs. of Turmeric.

2 lbs. of Blue Vitriol.

No. 13.

10 *Pieces,* ⅜ BROWN OLIVE.

Worsted Dye with 5 lbs. of Turmeric.
1 gill of Chemic.
10 lbs. of Super Argol.
1 quart of Oil of Vitriol.
Clean, Sumach, and Iron them separately, and
    spirit with
1 pint of Muriate of Tin.
Clean again, and Dye off with 2 lbs. of Logwood.
10 lbs. of Peachwood.
2½ lbs. of Blue Vitriol.

No. 14.

10 *Pieces,* ⅜ DARK GREEN.

Worsted Dye with 20 lbs. of Fustic.
3 pints of Chemic.
10 lbs. of Alum.
5 lbs. of Red Argol.

Clean, and dye the Cotton by first running them through Sumach, and then through Iron, clean again, and then run 8 ends through 10 lbs. of spent Logwood.

23

No. 15.

10 *Pieces*, $\frac{6}{4}$ INVISIBLE GREEN.

Worsted Dye same as No. 14, but add 1 quart more of Chemic.

Cotton Dye same as No. 14.

Dark Greens may be got from Chroming in White Warps as well as in Black.

No. 16.

10 *Pieces*, $\frac{6}{4}$ RED CLARET.

Prepare same as No. 4.

Chrome same as No. 7.

Finish with 20 lbs. of Peachwood.

$\frac{1}{2}$ lb. of Alum.

1 lb. of Logwood.

No. 17.

10 *Pieces*, $\frac{6}{4}$ RED BROWN.

Prepare same as No. 1.

Dye with 20 lbs. of Peachwood.

5 lbs. of Logwood.

10 lbs. of Turmeric.

$3\frac{1}{2}$ lbs. of Blue Vitriol.

2 lbs. of Alum.

No. 18.

10 *Pieces*, ⁹⁄₄ DARK BROWN.

Prepare same as No. 4.

Chrome same as No. 7.

Finish with 5 lbs. of Logwood.

10 lbs. of Peachwood.

10 lbs. of Fustic.

2½ lbs. of Alum.

No. 19.

10 *Pieces*, ⁹⁄₄ SILVER DRAB.

Worsted Dye with 4 spoonfuls of Liquid Extract.

½ handful of Cudbear.

10 lbs. of Super Argol.

3 gills of Oil of Vitriol.

Clean and Cotton Dye by first running them in Sumach and Iron, 8 ends separately, and then clear with 1 tot of Oil of Vitriol in a cistern of clean water.

No. 20.

10 *Pieces*, ⁹⁄₄ DARK SILVER DRAB.

Worsted Dye with 6 spoonfuls of Liquid Extract.

½ handful of Cudbear.

1 handful of Madder.

10 lbs. of Super Argol.

3 gills of Oil of Vitriol.

Cotton Dye same as No. 19.

No. 21.

10 *Pieces,* ¾ STONE DRAB.

Worsted Dye with 5 spoonfuls of Liquid Extract.
5 lbs. of Madder.
1 handful of Paste Cudbear.
10 lbs. of Super Argol.
3 gills of Oil of Vitriol.

Cotton Dye by running them in Sumach and Iron, 8 ends, and then through 2 pails of Catechu Liquor, and 1 tot of Oil of Vitriol.

No. 22.

10 *Pieces,* ¾ MADDER DRAB.

Worsted Dye with 5 spoonfuls of Liquid Extract.
10 lbs. of Madder.
10 lbs. of Super Argol.
1 handful of Paste Cudbear.
3 gills of Oil of Vitriol.

Cotton Dye by first running them in Sumach, and then in Iron, then through a cistern of warm water, with $\frac{1}{2}$ lb. of Chrome, melted, and 2 Buckets of Catechu Liquor.

No. 23.

10 *Pieces*, ⅘ LAVENDER DRAB.

First run 1 end in the Copperas Vat, then Worsted
  Dye in a clean vessel with 2 lbs. of White Argol.
2 lbs. of Alum.
8 spoonfuls of Paste Extract.

No. 24.

10 *Pieces*, ⅘ PINK.

Worsted Dye with 5 pints of Nitrate of Tin.
2 lbs. of White Argol.
5 ozs. of Dry Cochineal.
5 ozs. of Paste Cochineal.

Clean and Cotton Dye with 1 pint of Spent or
Bottled Safflower and 1 tot of Oil of Vitriol, in
a cistern of clean water.

No. 25.

10 *Pieces*, ⅘ SEA GREEN.

Worsted Dye with 10 lbs. of Fustic.
10 lbs. of Alum.
2 lbs. of White Argol.
2 tots of Liquid Extract.

Clean and Cotton Dye by running them 20
minutes in Nitrate of Iron, at 4° Twaddell, then

23*

run 6 ends through 1½ lb. of Prussiate of Potass in a vessel of cold water, then take up and add 1 gill of Oil of Vitriol, run 8 ends more and clean off.

No. 26.

10 *Pieces*, ⅘ SKY BLUE.

Worsted Dye with 1 tot of Liquid Extract.
10 lbs. of Crystals.
1 quart of Oil of Vitriol.
Cotton Dye same as No. 25.

No. 27.

10 *Pieces*, ⅘ FULL BLACK.

Boil 20 minutes with 2 lbs. of Chrome.
Sumach* them with 10 lbs. of Sumach.
Then Iron, clean, and finish with 50 lbs. of Logwood.
15 lbs. of Fustic.
1 lb. of Red Argol.

* A ½ lb. of Sumach is sufficient to a Piece when a quantity is Sumached together, but rather more must be used when only a few are Sumached together.

The Sumach may be used in Cold Water as well as in Warm, without being boiled up in the bottom of a cistern, as it generally leaves a redness on the face of the Piece.

COLORED MERINOS.

No. 1.

10 *Pieces*, ¼ ROYAL BLUE.

Heat up to 100°, add 10 lbs. of Prussiate, and 10 quarts of Blue Spirits, run half an hour, take up, heat up to 140°; but enter again and run another half hour, take up again and heat up to 180°, add 2 quarts of Finishing Spirits, enter again, and run another half hour, get out and cool over, heat up to the boiling point, add other 3 quarts of Finishing Spirits, enter again and boil half an hour, get out and clean off.

No. 2.

10 *Pieces*, ¼ DARK ROYAL BLUE.

Same as No. 1 in all respects, except half an hour's additional boiling, with 2 lbs. of Logwood, and another quart of Finishing Spirits as the last operation.

Lighter shades of No. 1 may be got by using less Prussiate, and darker than No. 2, by adding more Logwood.

No. 3.

10 *Pieces*, ¾ BLUE SHADE OF GRAIN MAROON.

Boil 20 minutes with 6 lbs. of Cudbear.
Then in a separate vessel boil half an hour with
2 quarts of Nitrate of Tin.
2 lbs. of White Argol.
1 lb. of Dry Cochineal.

———

No. 4.

10 *Pieces*, ¾ FULL GRAIN CRIMSON.

Boil half an hour with 4 lbs. of White Argol.
4 lbs. of Alum.
10 lbs. of Paste Cochineal.
8 lbs. of Dry Cochineal.
8 quarts of Spirits.

Nitrate of Tin is the Spirit for a Grain Color.

———

No. 5.

10 *Pieces*, ¾ LIGHT PINK.

Dye with 10 ozs. of Cochineal Paste.
4 ozs. of Dry Cochineal.
3 lbs. of Tartar.
6 quarts of Spirits.
Boil half an hour.

No. 6.

10 *Pieces*, ¼ SALMON.

Dye with 6 quarts of Spirits.
6 lbs. of Tartar.
½ lb. of Cochineal.
¼ lb. of Paste Cochineal.

Boil half an hour.

No. 7.

10 *Pieces*, ¼ GRAIN ROSE.

Dye with 6 quarts of Spirits.
4 lbs. of Tartar.
6 lbs. of Dry Cochineal.
2 lbs. of Paste Cochineal.

Boil half an hour.

No. 8.

10 *Pieces*, ¼ LIGHT ORANGE.

Dye with 8 lbs. of Young Fustic.
1¼ lb. of Dry Cochineal.
6 quarts of Spirits.
4 lbs. of Tartar.

Boil half an hour.

No. 9.

10 *Pieces*, ¾ YELLOW.

Dye with 4 lbs. of Tartar.
1 lb. of Alum.
5 quarts of Spirits.
7½ lbs. of Young Fustic.

Boil half an hour.

———

No. 10.

10 *Pieces*, ¾ GRAIN SCARLET.

Dye with 8 lbs. of Cochineal.
4 lbs. of Tartar.
8 quarts of Spirits.
3 lbs. of Young Fustic.

Boil half an hour.

———

No. 11.

10 *Pieces*, ¾ LAC SCARLET.

Dye with 4 lbs. of Tartar.
10 quarts of Spirits.
10 lbs. of good Lac.
8 lbs. of Young Fustic.

Boil 1 hour.

Either White or Brown Tartar will answer the purpose.

No. 12.

10 *Pieces*, ⅔ LIGHT PEA GREEN.

Dye with 10 lbs. of Alum.
5 lbs. of White Argol.
5 lbs. of Old Fustic.
6 spoonfuls of Liquid Extract.
Boil half an hour.

No. 13.

10 *Pieces*, ⅔ SEA GREEN.

Dye with 1 gill of Liquid Extract.
10 lbs. of Fustic.
5 lbs. of Argol.
20 lbs. of Alum.
Boil half an hour.

No. 14.

10 *Pieces*, ⅔ APPLE GREEN.

Dye with 1 gill of Liquid Extract.
5 lbs. of Red Argol.
10 lbs. of Turmeric.
3 pints of Oil of Vitriol.
Boil half an hour.

No. 15.

10 *Pieces*, ¾ BOTTLE GREEN.

Dye with 20 lbs. of Fustic.
20 lbs. of Alum.
10 lbs. of Red Argol.
3 pints of Chemic.

> Boil 1 hour.

No. 16.

10 *Pieces*, ¾ INVISIBLE GREEN.

Dye with 5 pints of Chemic.
10 lbs. of Super Argol.
10 lbs. of Alum.
½ a Dish of Logwood.

> Boil 1 hour.

No. 17.

10 *Pieces*, ¾ CHROMED GREEN.

Boil 20 minutes with 1 lb. of Chrome.
Finish with 20 lbs. of Fustic.
8 lbs. of Logwood.

> Boil half an hour in the finishing.

No. 18.

10 *Pieces*, ¾ CHROMED INVISIBLE GREEN.

Boil 20 minutes with 1 lb. of Chrome.
Finish with 15 lbs. of Fustic.
12 lbs. of Logwood.

Boil half an hour.

Compare the last two with Nos. 15 and 16, and you will see the difference of cost.

———

No. 19.

10 *Pieces*, ¾ PURPLE.

Chrome same as No. 17.
Finish with 3 lbs. of Logwood.
5 lbs. of Cudbear.
1 pint of Ammonia.

Boil half an hour.

———

No. 20.

10 *Pieces*, ¾ LIGHT CHROMED PURPLE.

Chrome same as No. 17.
Finish with 8 lbs. of Cudbear.
¼ lb. of Logwood.

Boil half an hour.

24

No. 21.

10 *Pieces*, ⁶/₄ VIOLET.

Boil 20 minutes with 10 lbs. of Cudbear.
Then run them through a Copperas Vat.

No. 22.

10 *Pieces*, ⁶/₄ RED RUBY.

Boil 20 minutes with 10 lbs. of Cudbear.
Then wash off.

No. 23.

10 *Pieces*, ⁶/₄ MAROON.

Boil 3 hours with 30 lbs. of Alum.
10 lbs. of Red Argol.
Clean well, and finish with 25 lbs. of Peachwood.
1 quart of Ammonia.
> Boil half an hour in the finishing.

No. 24.

10 *Pieces*, ⁶/₄ LIGHT CLARET.

Boil 3 hours with 30 lbs. of Alum.
10 lbs. of Red Argol.
Clean and finish with 20 lbs. of Peachwood.
1 gallon of Ammonia.
> Boil half an hour.

No. 25.

10 *Pieces*, ⅔ MIDDLE CLARET.

Boil 3 hours with 30 lbs. of Alum.
10 lbs. of Red Argol.
½ lb. of Logwood.
Clean and finish with 25 lbs. of Peachwood.
3 quarts of Ammonia.

Boil half an hour.

No. 26.

10 *Pieces*, ⅔ FULL CLARET.

Boil 3 hours with 30 lbs. of Alum.
10 lbs. of Red Argol.
3 lbs. of Logwood.
Clean and finish with 30 lbs. of Peachwood.
4 quarts of Ammonia.

Boil half an hour.

No. 27.

10 *Pieces*, ⅔ DARK GREEN OLIVE.

Dye with 10 lbs. of Turmeric.
1 quart of Chemic.
10 lbs. of Super Argol.
3 pints of Oil of Vitriol.

Boil 1 hour.

No. 28.

10 *Pieces,* $\frac{2}{4}$ BROWN OLIVE.

Dye with 10 lbs. of Turmeric.
15 lbs. of Camwood.
1 pint of Chemic.
3 pints of Oil of Vitriol.
10 lbs. of Super Argol.

Boil 1 hour.

No. 29.

10 *Pieces,* $\frac{2}{4}$ FULL RED BROWN.

Dye with 30 lbs. of Camwood.
3 gills of Chemic.
2 quarts of Oil of Vitriol.
4 lbs. of Turmeric.
10 lbs. of Super Argol.

Boil 1½ hour.

No. 30.

10 *Pieces,* $\frac{2}{4}$ DARK COFFEE BROWN.

Dye with 30 lbs. of Camwood.
5 lbs. of Turmeric.
3 pints of Chemic.
2 quarts of Oil of Vitriol.
10 lbs. of Super Argol.

Boil 1½ hour.

No. 31.

10 *Pieces*, ⁶⁄₄ ADELAIDE.

Chrome same as No. 17.
Finish with 3 lbs. of Cudbear.
10 lbs. of Peachwood.
2 lbs. of Logwood.
> Boil half an hour in the finishing.

———

No. 32.

10 *Pieces*, ⁶⁄₄ MULBERRY.

Chrome same as No. 17.
Finish with 10 lbs. of Cudbear.
10 lbs. of Peachwood.
10 lbs. of Logwood.
1 quart of Ammonia.
> Boil half an hour in the finishing.

———

No. 33.

10 *Pieces*, ⁶⁄₄ LIGHT SKY BLUE.

Dye with 2 quarts of Oil of Vitriol.
10 lbs. of Crystals.
10 spoonfuls of Liquid Extract.
> Boil 40 minutes.

24*

No. 34.

10 *Pieces*, ⅔ DARK SKY BLUE.

Dye with 2 quarts of Oil of Vitriol.
10 lbs. of Crystals.
1 gill of Liquid Extract.

Boil 40 minutes.

Where Bluer and more bloomy shades are required, add 1 oz. of Prussiate, and a cupful of
Nitrate of Tin to the 10 Pieces.

No. 35.

10. *Pieces*, ⅔ LAVENDER.

Dye with 1 quart of Oil of Vitriol.
10 lbs. of Crystals.
1 lb. of Paste Cudbear.
1 gill of Liquid Extract.

Boil 40 minutes.

No. 36.

10 *Pieces*, ⅔ RED LAVENDER.

Dye with 1 quart of Oil of Vitriol.
10 lbs. of Crystals.
2 lbs. of Paste Cudbear.
1 gill of Liquid Extract.

Boil 40 minutes.

No. 37.

10 *Pieces*, ⅔ MADDER DRAB.

Dye with 3 pints of Oil of Vitriol.
10 lbs. of Super Argol.
1 handful of Paste Cudbear.
4 spoonfuls of Liquid Extract.
5 lbs. of Madder.

Boil 1 hour.

No. 38.

10 *Pieces*, ⅔ FULL DRAB.

Dye with 3 pints of Oil of Vitriol.
10 lbs. of Super Argol.
1 handful of Paste Cudbear.
1 lb. of Madder.
3 spoonfuls of Liquid Extract.

Boil 1 hour.

No. 39.

10 *Pieces*, ⅔ SILVER DRAB.

Dye with 3 pints of Oil of Vitriol.
10 lbs. of Crystals.
3 spoonfuls of Liquid Extract.
½ a handful of Paste Cudbear.

Boil 40 minutes.

No. 40.

10 *Pieces*, ⁶⁄₄ BLUE BLACK.

Boil 20 minutes with 1¼ lb. of Chrome.
Finish with 20 lbs. of Logwood.
2 lbs. of Peachwood.
>   Boil half an hour in the finishing.

No. 41.

10 *Pieces*, ⁶⁄₄ FULL BLACK.

Boil half an hour with 1½ lb. of Chrome.
Finish with 30 lbs. of Logwood.
10 lbs. of Fustic.
1 lb. of Red Argol.
>   Boil half an hour in the finishing.

WOOLLEN SHAWL DYEING.

No. 1.

100 WOOLLEN SHAWLS.—ROYAL BLUE.

Dissolve 12 lbs. of Prussiate, and put it into a vessel with 2 quarts of Ammonia; run the Shawls 6 ends cold; take up, and add 12 quarts of Blue Spirits, and run 6 ends more cold; take up again, and heat up to 120°; then run 6 ends more; take up again, and heat up to 180°; then run 6 ends more, take them out, cool them over, add 3 pints of Finishing Spirits, and heat up to the boiling point; enter again, and boil half an hour; take them out, cool over, and add 3 pints more of Finishing Spirits; enter again, boil half an hour, and then clean off.

No. 2.

70 SHAWLS.—BLOOMY ROYAL BLUE.

Dissolve 12 lbs. of Prussiate, which put into a cistern of cold water, with 1½ lb. of Logwood and 9 quarts of Blue Spirits. Run 6 ends cold, then

take them up, and add 3 quarts more of Blue
Spirits; get down again, put the steam on with
the Shawls in the vessel, heat up to the boiling
point, and boil 20 minutes; then take out, cool
over, add 3 quarts of Finishing Spirits, boil up
well before entering them, enter, boil 20 minutes
more, and then clean off.

This is the best mode of dyeing Royal Blue
Shawls.

No. 3.

50 SHAWLS.—LIGHT ROSE.

Dye with 2½ lbs. of Alum.
5 lbs. of White Tartar.
4 quarts of Nitrate of Tin.
12 ozs. of Dry Cochineal.

Give them half the Cochineal at the beginning,
and the remainder when they have boiled half an
hour, after which boil half an hour more.

No. 4.

60 SHAWLS.—FULL ROSE.

Dye with 5 lbs. of Tartar.

2½ lbs. of Alum.

4 quarts of Spirits.

1½ lb. of Dry Cochineal.

Boil 40 minutes.

Less Spirits and Acid will do when shades of the same sort have been dyed before in the same vessel.

No. 5.

50 SHAWLS.—LIGHT SALMON.

Dye with 4 lbs. of Tartar.

2 ozs. of Young Fustic.

4 ozs. of Cochineal.

3 quarts of Spirits.

Boil 40 minutes.

No. 6.

30 SHAWLS.—FULL SALMON.

Dye with 3 lbs. of Tartar.

8 ozs. of Cochineal.

4 ozs. of Young Fustic.

3 pints of Spirits.

Boil 40 minutes.

No. 7.

40 SHAWLS.—MELON.

Dye with 8 ozs. of Cochineal.
3 lbs. of Tartar.
4 pints of Spirits.
> Boil 40 minutes.

—

No. 8.

40 SHAWLS.—YELLOW.

Dye with 3 lbs. of Tartar.
1 lb. of Alum.
3 lbs. of Quercitron Bark.
4 pints of Oxalic Tin.
> Boil 20 minutes.

—

No. 9.

40 SHAWLS.—ORANGE.

Dye with 4 lbs. of Tartar.
8 ozs. of Cochineal.
4 lbs. of Young Fustic.
4 pints of Spirits.
> Boil half an hour.

No. 10.

40 SHAWLS.—YELLOW BUFF.

Dye with 3 lbs. of Tartar.
5 pints of Spirits.
1 oz. of Cochineal.
2 ozs. of Young Fustic.
　　　　Boil half an hour.

———

No. 11.

40 SHAWLS.—LIGHT BUFF.

2 ozs. of Cochineal.
3 ozs. of Young Fustic.
2 lbs. of Tartar.
3 pints of Spirits.
　　　　Boil half an hour.

———

No. 12.

40 SHAWLS.—FULL BUFF.

Dye with 4 ozs. of Young Fustic.
3 lbs. of Tartar.
4 ozs. of Cochineal.
3 pints of Spirits.
　　　　Boil half an hour.

No. 13.

40 SHAWLS.—SCARLET.

Dye with 8 lbs. of good Lac.
4 lbs. of Tartar.
4 lbs. of Young Fustic.
3 pints of Nitrate of Tin.
6 pints of Oxalic Tin.

Boil 1 hour.

No. 14.

40 SHAWLS.—LAVENDER.

Dye with 3 lbs. of Tartar.
8 ozs. of Cudbear.
1 gill of Liquid Extract.

Boil half an hour.

No. 15.

40 SHAWLS.—SKY BLUE.

Dye with 10 lbs. of Common Crystals.
1 quart of Oil of Vitriol.
1 gill of Liquid Extract.

Boil half an hour.

ART OF PADDING.

TO MAKE THE STANDARD COLORS, AND HOW TO MIX THEM FOR VARIOUS SHADES.

———◆———

PADDING is only another mode of dyeing the same color. It is done by a Machine, rather similar to the Crabbing-Machine. The Standard Colors are made according to the annexed Receipts. In Padding any color, the liquor is put into the Trough, above which are two Rollers, which revolve against each other with great pressure; they are covered either with Woollen or Cotton, and the lower Roller revolves in the Dyeing Liquid. The pieces are put under the Trolly, or small Roller in the Trough, and passed through the Machine. Some light colors are dyed sufficiently by passing them only once through the Machine; while darker colors require to be passed through two or three times, adding more Dye Liquor according to shade. By means of Padding, Cotton and Worsted may be dyed nearly the same color at the same time, but colors

produced by Padding are not so permanent as
those obtained by the ordinary mode of dyeing.
A more permanent color by Padding may be got
by dyeing the Worsted first a little lighter than
the shade required, and then by Cotton Dyeing
by passing through the Padding-Machine. The
Pieces, after having been Padded, are taken to
the Drying-Machine, and dried off the Rolls, or
passed slowly through a hot stove. Any person
not acquainted with padding may soon acquire the
art, and produce equally as good colors as any
person who has been practising for some time, by
adopting the following Receipts, which show how
to make the Standard Colors, and how they are
mixed. It is difficult, however, to convey to any
person not acquainted with matching, the nicety
of bringing up the particular hue required. It
can be obtained only by practice.

N. B.—Though there are many different colors
or tints in the works of nature, and also in objects
produced by art, yet all the colors that we see, or
can imagine, are formed of only three colors,
called the *primary colors*, viz., red, yellow, and
blue. All other colors are mixed in different ways
from these, and are denominated *compound colors*.
Hence *Green* is a mixture of yellow and blue;
and the shade may be varied by taking more of
the one and less of the other. *Orange* is a mixture of yellow and red; *purple*, a mixture of blue

and red; and *violet* is obtained by the addition of more blue to the mixture. Brown, drab, gray, lilac, and other colors or tints, are also formed by similarly mixing the primary colors. White is perfect lightness, or the absence of all color, and black is perfect darkness. White and black, strictly speaking, are not colors, though they are seen both in nature and art.

25*

RECEIPTS FOR PADDING.

———•———

No. 1.

ESTARIAZER STANDARD.

4½ gallons of Water.
1 gallon of Brown Standard.
1 gallon of Red Liquor.
1 quart of Iron Liquor, 24° Twaddell.
2 quarts of Logwood Liquor, 8° Twaddell.
1 pint of Bark Liquor, 8° Twaddell.

To pad this color, give Water according to shade.

———

No. 2.

RED BROWN STANDARD.

8 gallons of Sapan Liquor, 8° Twaddell.
8 gallons of Bark Liquor, 12° Twaddell.
8 gallons of Fustic Liquor, 8° Twaddell.
24 lbs. of Alum.
6 lbs. of Sugar of Lead.

Dissolve together, and, when settled, use the clear Liquor only; dissolve 6 lbs. of Verdigris in

2 gallons of Water, 4 gallons of Purple Standard. Mix together.

As this grows better by keeping, it should be prepared three or four weeks before it is used.

No. 3.

DARK PURPLE STANDARD.

4 gallons of Red Liquor.
8 lbs. of Logwood, heat up to 120°.
Add ¼ lb. of Oxalic Acid.

Let it settle 24 hours, and use the clear liquor only.

No. 4.

DRAB STANDARD.

2 quarts of Bark Liquor, 10° Twaddell.
2 quarts of Iron Liquor, 24° Twaddell.
2 gallons of Water.
1 pint of Gall Liquor, 10° Twaddell.

No. 5.

DRAB STANDARD.

3 quarts of Bark Liquor, 10° Twaddell.
1 noggin of Acetic Acid.
1 noggin of Carbonate of Iron.

To 1 gallon of this Standard add Water according to shade.

No. 6.

GRAY, OR QUAKER DRAB STANDARD.

1 lb. of Copperas, dissolve in 8 quarts of hot
Water.

2 quarts of Gall Liquor, 4° Twaddell.

1 gill of Sulphate of Indigo, or Chemic.

———

No. 7.

SLATE STANDARD.

½ lb. of Copperas.

5 quarts of hot Water.

1 gill of Chemic.

1 pint of Gall Liquor, 4° Twaddell.

1 quart of Iron Liquor.

———

No. 8.

DOVE STANDARD, OLD WAY.

1 gallon of Purple Standard.

1 pint of Extract of Indigo.

1 pint of Prussiate Liquor at 2 lbs. per gallon of
Water.*

1, 2, or 3 gallons of Water to 1 of the Standard,
as the shade may require.

* For the Prussiate Liquor, dissolve 2 lbs. of Prussiate
in 1 gallon of hot Water; and for the Extract of Indigo,
mix 1 quart of Sulphate of Indigo with 1 gallon of Water.

No. 9.

DARK DOVE STANDARD, NEW WAY.

4 pints of Gall Liquor, 5° Twaddell.
½ lb. of Copperas.
1 pint of Purple Standard.
1 noggin of Extract of Indigo.
1 noggin of Prussiate Liquor,* same as No. 8.

———

No. 10.

LIGHT DOVE STANDARD.

1 gallon of Purple Standard.
1 gallon of Water.
5 gills of Extract of Indigo.
3 gills of Prussiate Liquor.

———

No. 11.

FAWN DRAB STANDARD.

3 lbs. of Madder.
4 gallons of Water, boil 10 minutes.
Add ½ lb. of Alum.
5 gills of Iron Liquor.

* See note on previous page.

No. 12.

LAVENDER STANDARD.

10 gallons of hot Water.
½ lb. of Prussiate.
7 quarts of Purple Standard.
4 gills of Extract of Indigo.

———

No. 13.

SULPHATE OF INDIGO.

Take Sulphate of Indigo, or Chemic, dissolve
1½ lb. of ground Spanish Indigo in 6 lbs. of Sulphuric Acid, or Oil of Vitriol. Let it stand 24
hours in a warm Bath, then add 3 gallons of boiling water and 1 lb. of White Sugar of Lead, and
strain through flannel.

———

No. 14.

BLUE STANDARD.

4 quarts of hot Water.
¼ lb. of Oxalic Acid.
1 pint of Prussiate Liquor.
1 pint of Extract.
When bloom is wanted, add a little Bloom Pink
Standard.

No. 15.

BLOOM PINK STANDARD.

1 lb. of Cochineal and 2 lbs. of Spirits of Ammonia; mix and let them stand in a warm place 24 hours, and then add 2 gallons of Water; boil down to 1 gallon, then add 12 ozs. of Alum, ¼ a pound of Oxalic Acid, ½ a pound of Tin Crystals.

No. 16.

ROYAL BLUE STANDARD.

3 gallons of warm Water.
8 lbs. of Prussiate of Potash.
6 lbs. of Tartaric Acid.
6 quarts of Prussiate of Tin.
1 gill of Blue Spirits.
This will do either for padding or printing.

No. 17.

PRUSSIATE OF TIN.

To make Prussiate of Tin dissolve 4 lbs. of Prussiate of Potash in 6 gallons of warm Water; in another vessel dissolve 5 lbs. of Tin Crystals in 6 gallons of Water, and mix both liquors together; then pour cold Water into the admixture, when the Prussiate will be precipitated, forming a pulp at the bottom of the vessel. Pour cold Water upon it till all the acid be washed off. The result will be two gallons of pulp, which will be the real Prussiate of Tin.

No. 18.

CLARET STANDARD.

5 gallons of Sapan Liquor, 8° Twaddell.
4 gallons of Logwood Liquor, 8° Twaddell.
1½ lb. of Sal Ammoniac.
　Mix well, and let them stand 24 hours.

No. 19.

TO PAD CLARET.

Take 8 gallons of Claret Standard.
4 gallons of Red Liquor.
3 pints of Extract of Indigo.
3 pints of Nitrate of Copper.
3 lbs. of Common Salt.

No. 20.

TO PAD BLACK.

1 gallon of Logwood Liquor, 8° Twaddell.
1 pint of Pyroligneous Acid, 4° Twaddell.
½ a noggin of Acetate of Copper.
1 noggin of Nitrate of Iron.
1 noggin of Muriate of Iron.
1 noggin of Extract of Indigo.

No. 21.

TO MAKE ACETATE OF COPPER.

Dissolve 4 lbs. of Sulphate of Copper, or Blue Vitriol, and 2 lbs. of Sugar of Lead in 1 gallon of boiling Water.

No. 22.

STONE DRAB STANDARD.

Dissolve in 4 gallons of hot Water 1 lb. of Copperas.
Add 4 pints of Gall Liquor, 4° Twaddell.
4 pints of Bark Liquor, 2° Twaddell.
1 pint of Nitrate of Iron.
1 noggin of Sulphate of Indigo, or Chemic.
Add Water according to shade required.

26

No. 23.

ORANGE STANDARD.

4 gallons of Water.
6 lbs. of Annotta.
¼ lb. of Pearlash.
½ lb. of Soft Soap.
   Boil 10 minutes and let it settle 12 hours.

———

No. 24.

LIGHT OLIVE STANDARD.

1 quart of Bark Liquor, 10° Twaddell.
1 quart of Fustic Liquor, 8° Twaddell.
1 quart of Red Liquor.
1 quart of Purple Standard.
1 quart of Logwood Liquor, 8° Twaddell.

———

No. 25.

TO PAD DARK SHADES OF OLIVE.

Use 2 quarts of Bark Liquor, 10° Twaddell.
12 quarts of Fustic Liquor, 12° Twaddell.
1 lb. of Alum.
2 quarts of Purple Standard.
Logwood Liquor according to shade.

No. 26.

LILAC.

Take 2 quarts of Pink Standard.
4 quarts of Purple Standard.

No. 27.

SLATE STANDARD.

2 lbs. of Copperas.
2 gallons of hot Water.
2 quarts of Gall Liquor, 10° Twaddell.
2 quarts of Sulphate of Indigo.
Add water according to shade.

No. 28.

FIRST SHADE, YELLOW STONE DRAB.

4 quarts of Bark Liquor, 2° Twaddell.
4 gallons of Water.
1 quart of Gall Liquor.
2 quarts of Iron Liquor.

No. 29.

SECOND SHADE, STONE DRAB.

4 quarts of Bark Liquor, 2° Twaddell.
1 pint of Iron Liquor.
½ a noggin of Sulphate of Indigo.
Add water according to shade.

No. 30.

THIRD SHADE.

1 quart of Bark Liquor, 2° Twaddell.
1 noggin of Iron Liquor.
3 quarts of First Shade Standard.

No. 31.

CINNAMON STANDARD.

1 gallon of Water.
2 lbs. of Annotta.
1 lb. of Pearlash.
Boil together.
In another vessel, boil 2 lbs. of Catechu.
1 gallon of Water.
1 lb. of Chrome.
1 pint of Acetate of Copper.

No. 32.

TO PAD CINNAMON.

Use 1 pint of Acetate of Copper.
1 gallon of Cinnamon Standard.
Half out of each vessel, as described in No. 31.

No. 33.

TO PAD ESTARIAZER COLOR.

2 gallons of Cinnamon Standard.
1 gallon of No. 28, Stone Standard.
1 quart of Logwood Liquor, 8° Twaddell.

No. 34.

TO PAD SLATE COLORS.

Take 2 gallons of Slate Standard, No. 27.
4 gallons of Water.
Darker or Lighter Shades may be got by adding
more or less of the Standard.

No. 35.

DARK GREEN STANDARD.

1 gallon of Persian Berry Liquor, 16° Twaddell,
3 lbs. of Prussiate of Potash.
½ lb. of Oxalic Acid.
1 quart of Red Liquor.
3 gills of Extract of Indigo.
1 noggin of Muriate of Tin.
½ a noggin of Oil of Vitriol.

26*

No. 36.

PALE GREEN.

2 quarts of Green Standard, No. 35.
1 pint of Persian Berry Liquor.
And water as required.

———

No. 37.

SKY BLUE STANDARD.

Mix 10 lbs. of good Paste Extract with 1 pailful of Water; dissolve every particle to prevent Blotches when used; fill the Trough to a little above the Trolly, then add 1 quart of this Standard for a Light Blue, and 1 gill of Ammonia, and boil while running the first end through; if not dark enough, run through again. For Dark Shades add more Extract and Ammonia.

———

No. 38.

LAVENDER STANDARD.

Dissolve 20 lbs. of Alum and 10 lbs. of Sugar of Lead in 5 pails of Water, then take off the clear Liquor and heat up to 180°, and then put into a bag 4 or 5 pailfuls of Logwood, and rinse it in this Liquor; let it steep in it about 5 hours, and then draw out the bag. This is Lavender Bloom Standard.

For the Blue Standard for Lavenders, dissolve 3 lbs. of Tartaric Acid, 2 lbs. of Alum, and 14 lbs. of good Extract, with 2 pailfuls of hot Water. For Lighter or Darker Shades of Lavenders, take more or less of the Blue Standard with Bloom Standard, according to shade required.

TO PAD TEN PIECES, LAVENDER.

Take 1 pail of Bloom Standard and 2 quarts of Blue Standard, heat up to 180°, add 1 pint of Red Liquor, and then run 4 ends.

No. 39.

DRAB PREPARATION, OR ANOTHER MODE OF PADDING DRAB.

Take 3 pints of Fustic Liquor, 8° Twaddell, 1 pint of Muriate of Tin, run them 2 ends through the boiling Liquor at the Machine.

This mode of padding Drabs is preferred by some parties.

No. 40.

TO PAD DIFFERENT SHADES OF DRAB.

Fill up a little above the Trolly with cold Water, and put in a little Iron Liquor at full strength, a little Blue Standard, a little Lavender Bloom

Standard, and a little Archil, all at full strength, according to shade required. For Fawn Shades, add only a little Bloom, but for heavier shades add a little Iron Liquor as well; for Bluer shades of Drab, add a little Blue Standard; and for very blooming shades, add a little Archil with more Bloom Standard. With more or less of these Ingredients properly mixed, any shade of Drab may be got without much difficulty, the Goods being previously prepared according to No. 39, it being the basis for all these Ingredients.

No. 41.

SKY BLUE.

Another mode of Padding.—Take 6 gallons of Water, 1½ noggin of Nitrate of Iron 90° Twaddell, ½ a noggin of Muriate of Tin, mix well, run 3 ends, then dissolve 4 ozs. of Tartaric Acid, and 4 ozs. of Yellow Prussiate of Potash, in 6 gallons of Water, to which add ½ a noggin of Extract of Indigo, and put this into the Trough, and run 3 or 4 ends according to shade required, and then dry at the Machine.

No. 42.

ROYAL BLUE.

How to prepare Royal Blues.—Add 3 lbs. of Tin Crystals to 1 pint of Oil of Vitriol; in another vessel, melt 4 lbs. of Chloride of lime, add 1 gill of Oil of Vitriol with 8 gallons of Water, run 4 ends through Tin Preparation 6° Twaddell, then through the Chloride of Lime 2° Twaddell, then through a fresh Liquor of Nitrate of Iron 12° Twaddell, then through Soda, 1½ lb. to a Piece; wash and run them in strong Prussiate Liquor, with a little Oil of Vitriol in it, at the Padding-Machine, after which they must be steamed.

The Steaming will raise the Cotton and the Worsted from a flat Green to a good Blue.

SILK WARP, SKEIN,

AND

HANDKERCHIEF PRINTING.

No. 1.—BLACK.

3 gallons of Logwood Liquor, 8° Twaddell; 3 lbs. of D. British Gum, 12 oz. of Gum Dragon, 6 ozs. of Sal Ammoniac, boil well. When half cold, add 1 pint of S. Copper Liquor. When cold, add 1 quart of Muriate of Iron, 3 gills of Nitrate of Iron.

No. 2.—SCARLET.

1 gallon of Cochineal Liquor, 8° Twaddell, 1 lb. of Starch. At blood heat, add 3 ozs. of Oxalic Acid, 4 ozs. of Tin Crystals, 1 gill of Persian Berry Liquor, 8° Twaddell.

No. 3.—GREEN.

1 gallon of French Berry Liquor, 8° Twaddell, 1 lb. of Alum, 1 lb. of Flour. When taken off the fire, add 1 quart of Extract of Indigo, 1 quart of Red Liquor.

No. 4.—CLARET.

1 quart of Bronze Logwood, 1 quart of Bronze Peachwood, 1 quart of Red Liquor, 2½ lbs. of British Gum. When taken off the fire, add 1 quart of V. Copper Liquor.

No. 5.—BROWN.

10 parts of Amber Color, 4 parts of Ruby, 1 part of Black.

No. 6.—DARK RED.

8 of Bronze Peachwood, 1 of Nitromuriate of Tin, add 2 of the above to 1 of Gum Water, then add 1 lb. of Alum per gallon.

No. 7.—ORANGE.

3 lbs. of good Annotta, 1 lb. of Caustic Potash, 16° Twaddell. Boil until dissolved, add 1 of the above to 2 of Gum Water, and then add 2 ozs. of Alum per gallon.

No. 8.—AMBER.

1 gallon of Berry Liquor, 9° Twaddell, 1 oz. of Alum, 2½ lbs. of British Gum. When taken off the fire, add 8 ozs. of Tin Crystals.

No. 9.—PINK.

1 lb. of fine ground Cochineal, 1 lb. of strong Spirits of Ammonia. Mix, and let them remain in a hot stove for at least 24 hours, then add 2 gallons of Water, and boil the whole down to 2 gallons, then add 4 ozs. of Alum, 4 ozs. of Oxalic Acid, 4 ozs. of Tin Crystals. Thicken with Gum Senegal.

No. 10.—LIGHT PINK.

1 of the above to 3 of Gum Water.

No. 11.—PEACH.

20 of Ammoniacal Cochineal, 1 of Extract of Indigo.

No. 12.—LIGHT PEACH.

1 of the above to 8 of Gum Water.

No. 13.—DARK PURPLE.

1 of Bronze Logwood, 1 of Red Liquor, 4 of Gum Water.

No. 14.—LIGHT PURPLE.

1 of Bronze Logwood, 5 of Red Liquor, 5 of Gum Water.

No. 15.—BLUE.

1 gallon of Red Liquor, 8 ozs. of Oxalic Acid, 4 ozs. of Tartaric Acid, 1 lb. of Paste Indigo. Thicken with Gum Senegal.

No. 16.—DARK BROWN.

26 quarts of Berry Liquor, 12° Twaddell, 10 quarts of Logwood Liquor, 12° Twaddell, 9 quarts of Sapan Liquor, 12° Twaddell, 5 lbs. of Sulphate of Copper, 10 lbs. of Alum, 2 lbs. of Salammoniac, 6 gallons of thick Gum Water.

No. 17.—LIGHT BROWN.

2 gallons of Catechu, 10° Twaddell, 1 gallon of Berry Liquor, 10° Twaddell, 1 gallon of Sapan Liquor, 6° Twaddell, 4 ozs. of Nitrate of Copper. Thicken with Gum Senegal.

No. 18.—POPPY RED.

2 lbs. of Ground Cochineal, 1 pint of Strong Ammonia, 3 pints of Water, 4 pints of Thick Gum Water, 4 ozs. of Alum, 4 ozs. of Oxalic Acid, 1 noggin of Muria-Sulphate of Tin. Pass the above through a fine Sieve.

27

No. 19.—DARK FAWN.

1 quart of Water, 1 pint of Berry Liquor, 12° Twaddell, 1 pint of Logwood Liquor, 8° Twaddell, 4 ozs. of Sal Ammoniac, 2 lbs. of Catechu, when dissolved, add 1 pint of V. Copper Liquor, thicken with British Gum.

No. 20.—LIGHT FAWN.

Take one of the above to 4 of Gum Water.

No. 21.—DARK DRAB.

1 quart of Logwood, 12° Twaddell, 1 quart of Sumach, 6° Twaddell, 2 quarts of Berry Liquor, 12° Twaddell, 4 ozs. of Alum, 2 quarts of Copperas Buff, thicken with British Gum.

No. 22.—LIGHT DRAB.

Add 2 of the above to 4 of Gum Water.

No. 23.—DARK DAHLIA.

1 gallon of Red Archil, 1 gallon of Sapan Liquor, 8° Twaddell, 6 lbs. of Gum Senegal, raise in a weak Ammonia Liquor.

No. 24.—LIGHT DAHLIA.

Add 1 of the above to 4 of Gum Water.

No. 25.—DARK BLUE.

2 quarts of Water, 2 lbs. of Prussiate of Potash, when dissolved, add 2 quarts of Gum Water, 4 ozs. of Tartaric Acid; when cold, add $\frac{1}{2}$ a noggin of Sulphuric Acid.

No. 26.—LIGHT BLUE.

In 1 gallon of Gum Water dissolve 2 ozs. of Tartaric Acid, and then add 1 pint of Extract of Indigo.

No. 27.—DARK GREEN.

1 gallon of Berry Liquor, 12° Twaddell, 12 ozs. of Alum, 2 lbs. of Prussiate of Potash, 4 ozs. of Oxalic Acid, when dissolved, thicken with 3 lbs. of Gum Senegal, 3 noggins of Vinegar; add 1 noggin of Muriate of Tin, stirring it well while adding it, to which add 1 quart of Extract of Indigo.

No. 28.—LIGHT GREEN.

Add 1 of the above to 3 of Gum Water.

No. 29.—SLATE STANDARD.

5 quarts of Red Liquor, 18° Twaddell, 1 gill of Iron Liquor, 22° Twaddell, add 5 parts of the above to 1 of Bronze Logwood, add 2 parts of the´ above Standard to 1 of Gum Water, for the Dark Slate Color.

No. 30.—LIGHT SLATE COLOR.

Add 1 of the Standard to 8 of Gum Water.

No. 31.—RED RUBY.

1 gallon of Bronze Peachwood, 3 lbs. of Gum Senegal, 1 lb. of Ground Alum, at blood heat, add 1 gill of Oxymuriate of Tin.

No. 32.—MAZE.

7 pints of Water, 3 ozs. of Pearlash, $1\frac{1}{2}$ lb. of Annotta.

No. 33.—DARK LAVENDER.

1 of Dark Purple, No. 13, 1 of Blue, No. 15, 2 of Gum Water.

No. 34.—LIGHT LAVENDER.

1 of Dark Purple, No. 13, 1 of Blue, No. 15, 6 of Gum Water.

No. 35.—DARK MAROON.

1 quart of Bronze Logwood, 1 quart of Bronze Peachwood, 1 quart of V. Copper Liquor. Thicken with 3 lbs. of British Gum. Boil well, and then add 1 quart of Red Liquor at 18° Twaddell.

No. 36.—LIGHT MAROON.

2 quarts of Catechu Liquor, 10° Twaddell, 2 quarts of Sumach Liquor, 6° Twaddell, thicken with Gum Senegal, and then add 6 ozs. of Nitromuriate of Tin.

No. 37.—DARK GRAIN CRIMSON.

1 lb. of ground Cochineal, 2 quarts of Spirits of Ammonia, mix and put in a hot stove for 24 hours, then add 2 quarts of water, and boil well; thicken with 3 lbs. of Gum Senegal, and then add 8 ozs. of Alum.

27*

No. 38.—PONTIA.

1 gallon of Cochineal Liquor, 8° Twaddell, thicken with 1 lb. of Starch, at blood heat, add 2 ozs. of Alum, 2 ozs. of Oxalic Acid, and 2½ ozs. of Crystals of Tin.

No. 39.—ROSE.

1 lb. of Ammoniacal Cochineal to 3 lbs. of Gum Water.

No. 40.—DARK APRICOT.

1 gallon of Water, 4 lbs. of Catechu, 8 ozs. of Sal Ammoniac, 1 pint of Sapan Liquor, 8° Twaddell, thicken with British Gum, add 1 pint of Copper Liquor, 1 gill of Muriate of Copper, and 1 pint of Red Liquor.

No. 41.—LIGHT APRICOT.

2 quarts of Persian Berry Liquor, 8° Twaddell, 6 ozs. of Alum, 1 quart of Maze Color, No. 32, 1 noggin of Oxymuriate of Tin, 2 quarts of Gum Water.

No. 42.—DARK RED PURPLE.

3 quarts of Bronze Logwood, 12 ozs. of Alum, for the Standard. For the Color, use 2 of Standard to 1 of Red Liquor and 3 of Gum Water.

No. 43.—LIGHT RED PURPLE.

1 of Standard, 1 of Red Liquor, and 6 of Gum Water.

No. 44.—DARK ORANGE.

5 quarts of Caustic Pearlash, 8° Twaddell, 2½ lbs. of Annotta, boil well, then 2 quarts of Water, boil again, then add 2 ozs. of Tartaric Acid, and 2 ozs. of Alum; thicken with 3 lbs. of British Gum.

No. 45.—LIGHT ORANGE.

1 of the above to 3 of Gum Water.

No. 46.—DARK OLIVE.

1 quart of Dark Purple Standard, No. 13, 1 quart of Bark and Fustic Liquor, 12° Twaddell, 1 pint of Blue, No. 15, 1 pint of Iron Liquor, 22° Twaddell, ½ a noggin of Extract of Indigo, 4 quarts of Gum Water.

No. 47.—LIGHT OLIVE.

1 of Dark Olive, No. 47, 4 of Gum Water, and 1 pint of Bark Liquor per gallon.

No. 48.—DARK CINNAMON BRONZE.

1 gallon of Cochineal Liquor, 4° Twaddell, 6 quarts of Persian Liquor, 8° Twaddell, 8 ozs. of Paste Extract of Indigo, mix very well, thicken with 5½ lbs. of British Gum, when off the fire add 8 ozs. of Tin Crystals, when nearly cold add 8 ozs. of Oxalic Acid.

No. 49.—LIGHT CINNAMON BROWN.

Add 1 of the above, No. 48, to 3 of Gum Water.

No. 50.—DARK YELLOW.

2 gallons of Persian Berry Liquor, 12° Twaddell, 8 ozs. of Tin Crystals, boil well, thicken with 1 lb. of British Gum and 1 lb. of Flour; when off the fire, add 8 ozs. of Salt.

No. 51.—LIGHT YELLOW.

2 quarts of Gum Water, 1 quart of Bark Liquor, 8° Twaddell, 1 quart of Red Liquor, 18° Twaddell, 4 ozs. of Cream of Tartar.

No. 52.—ORANGE BROWN.

2 quarts of Red Archil, 4 gallons of Yellow Color.

To make the Yellow Color.—1 gallon of Persian Berry Liquor, 12° Twaddell, 12 ozs. of Alum, 1 gill of Oxymuriate of Tin, 4 quarts of thick Gum Water.

No. 53.—LIGHT ORANGE BROWN.

1 quart of Red Archil, 6 quarts of Yellow Color.

No. 54.—HOW TO MAKE BRONZE PEACHWOOD.

1 gallon of Peachwood Liquor, 8° Twaddell, 8 ozs. of Sal Ammoniac; when cold, add 1 pint of Sulphate of Copper.

No. 55.—BRONZE LOGWOOD.

1 gallon of Logwood, 8° Twaddell, 8 ozs. of Sal Ammoniac; when dissolved, add 1 pint of Copper Liquor.

No. 56.—COPPER LIQUOR.

1 gallon of Water, 4 lbs. of Sulphate of Copper, 4 lbs. of Sugar of Lead; use only the clear Liquor.

———

No. 57.—ANNOTTA LIQUOR.

1 gallon of Caustic Potash, 5° Twaddell, 1½ lb. of Annotta, and boil until dissolved.

———

No. 58.—COPPERAS BUFF.

1 gallon of Water, 4 lbs. of Copperas, 8 ozs. of Sugar of Lead; use only the clear Liquor.

———

No. 59.—AMMONIACAL COCHINEAL.

2 lbs. of fine ground Cochineal, 5 pints of strong Ammonia, put in a close jar, and place it in a warm bath, or put it in a hot stove for 24 hours; then add 2 gallons of Water and boil it down to two gallons, to which add 4 ozs. of Alum, 4 ozs. of Oxalic Acid, and 4 ozs. of Tin Crystals.

———

No. 60.—EXTRACT OF INDIGO, FOR PRINTING.

Add 3 lbs. of Paste Extract to 1 gallon of Water.

No. 61.—DARK PRUSSIATE LIQUOR.

2 gallons of Water, 8 lbs. of Prussiate, 8 lbs. of Tartaric Acid, and 1 noggin of Sulphate of Indigo.

———

No. 62.—SULPHATE OF INDIGO.

Add 1 lb. of good Indigo to 4 lbs. of Sulphuric Acid (Oil of Vitriol).

HOW TO SET COPPERAS VATS.

HOW TO SET A COPPERAS VAT FOR DYEING COTTON WARPS AND HANKS.

In a half pipe tub of cold water, add 12 lbs. of ground Indigo; the Indigo must be ground in a barrel with water. To this add 12 lbs. of new slaked Lime and 24 lbs. of Copperas. Stir well a few times, and in the course of 24 hours it will be ready for use.

This will be a good vat, and will dye a great quantity of Cotton. It will dye a very good shade of Blue by passing the Cotton once through, and darker shades by passing through again. When the vat is nearly worn out, add to it a few pounds of Copperas, and a pound or two of Potash, which will revive it again. By this means all the strength of the Indigo may be got out of it. Some Dyers use considerably more Copperas in the setting, but this is enough when very bright shades are required.

HOW TO SET A COPPERAS VAT FOR PIECE DYEING.

In a large vat add 20 lbs. of Indigo, well ground as before, 100 lbs. of Copperas, and 30 lbs. of new slaked Lime. Stir well for half an hour until it has a Yellow appearance, and in the course of 24 hours it will be ready for use. After working the vat for some length of time, add a little more Copperas.

28

A SHORT DESCRIPTION OF DYEWARES MENTIONED IN THIS WORK.

ALUM.—This salt is prepared from certain clays containing pyrites. It is used very extensively in dyeing, in consequence of the attraction which Alumina has for coloring matter. It is used as a mordant or base for Mock Crimson, Maroon, Claret, Purple, &c., as may be seen in the foregoing receipts. However, in the dyeing of colors generally, Bichromate of Potass supersedes the use of Alum, being less injurious to the fabric, and giving a greater depth of color, and requiring smaller quantities of Dyewoods for the same shade. Alum is sometimes used after chroming, when the color is too full, being made lighter by adding a little. When the shade is too Blue, a little Alum will redden it.

ANNOTTA.—This is obtained from an American tree, called *bixa orellana*, and it is imported in the form of a paste, of a brick red color. It is soluble, or spent by Pearlash at boiling heat. It is used in dyeing various colors upon Cotton and Silks, viz: Buff, Salmon, Flat Yellow, Orange, and some Fawn shades of Drab. The colors may be raised by running in weak Nitric or Sulphuric Acid.

ARCHIL.—This is a Blue-red or Violet paste obtained from the *Lichen rocella*, grown in the south of France, and in the Canary Islands, where the best is produced. Alone it produces a Ruby color, and a very light Violet by adding a little Ammonia, or other alkalies. It reddens Indigo Blues, and combined with Logwood produces Purple.

AMMONIA.—Liquid Ammonia is generally distilled from Gas Liquor; it is sometimes made from Ammoniacal salts and Lime, but the best for dyeing purposes is made from Urine. It is very much used by Dyers for the purpose of blueing Crimsons, Clarets, Purples, &c. It is also used in making Paste Cochineal. See Receipt No. 31, Worsted Yarn Dyeing.

ARGOL.—It is obtained from the juice of the grape, and is a crystallized incrustation generally found in Wine Casks. It becomes white when purified by solution and crystallization, and is then called Cream of Tartar. In dyeing, Argol, combined with Alum, is generally used in the preparation or boiling of Mock Crimsons, Maroons, Clarets, and Purples. It is excellent in giving solidity to these and other colors. Being a weak Acid, it is the best for dyeing bright Greens, working well with Extract, Sulphate of Indigo, and is not destructive to Fustic. It is frequently used in dyeing the Spirit colors, as Scarlet, Orange, and Grain Crimson; but Cream of Tartar is preferable for Yellows, Pinks, Salmons, and other light Spirit colors.

SUPER ARGOL.—It is made from Sal-enixen, or Sulphate of Soda, and sometimes from common Salt-cake. As an acid, it is used for dyeing Drabs, and Greens when Turmeric is used instead of Fustic. Also for Olives and Browns. It is much cheaper than either Argol or Brown Tartar, and in some cases is preferable.

CAMWOOD.—This is a dark red Wood, containing strong coloring matter which is of a permanent nature, and is generally used for dying Browns and Olives upon Worsted Goods It is most soluble in Sulphuric Acid diluted with water. In the dyeing of Woollens, it is sometimes employed as a substitute for Red Saunders, producing a more fiery appearance in Browns of light and middle shades.

CATECHU.—Catechu is an extract from the heart-wood of the *Khair Tree* of the East Indies. The coloring matter is sometimes extracted by Sulphate of Copper, and sometimes by Nitrate of Copper; but Bichromate of Potass is a more efficient extractor of this color.   It is used in dyeing Cotton a variety of shades, varying from a Light Drab to a Dark Brown.

COCHINEAL.—Is a small Mexican Insect, containing strong coloring matter, very permanent.   It is used in dyeing Pinks, Rose colors, Oranges, Scarlets, and Crimsons.   The mode of extracting the coloring matter is by means of Nitrate of Tin, and Muriate of Tin; Oxalic Tin gives the brightest color. These Acids, for bright shades, are combined with White or Brown Tartar.

CHROME, OR BICHROMATE OF POTASS.—This is a red orange Crystal, and is of very great use as a mordant in dyeing Blacks and other dark colors upon Worsted and Woollen Goods, giving greater permanence than any other mordant previously employed.   Its excellent properties, in this respect, have only of late been appreciated, and it is now becoming generally used. The Author of this work unhesitatingly affirms that he was the first person, in the neighborhood of Halifax, to dye colors from Bichromate of Potass.   It effects a great saving of time and expense, &c.

CUDBEAR (see ARCHIL).—Cudbear is a dry powder, of a fine Blue-red color, and will dye a Ruby of itself, either upon Silk, Worsted, or Woollen; a Violet, with a little Logwood; a Purple or Adelaide; by previously undergoing the Chroming process. See Receipts Nos. 6 and 7, Orleans from Black Warps.   It is used in dyeing Lavenders, Drabs, and various other shades, for the red part of the color.

CHEMIC, OR SULPHATE OF INDIGO.—This is a blue paste prepared from Indigo, and contains more of it in solution than any other preparation of it whatever.   For Dyeing purposes, it is thus made: Put into a Stone Jar 36 lbs. of Sulphuric Acid, to which add 12 lbs. of ground Indigo gradually; stir well for 1 hour.   After standing a few hours, it will be fit for use.   This Chemic is much cheaper than Extract of Indigo for dyeing some colors, as Greens, Olives, and Browns.   Extracts of Indigo are only modifications of this Chemic, being partly neutralized and filtered.

FRENCH BERRY, OR PERSIAN BERRY.—This is the fruit of the *Rhamnus Infectorius.* They yield a bright Yellow coloring matter, which is employed in dyeing light Yellow shades upon Cotton; also for light Greens, with either Extract of Indigo or Prussiate of Potass. They also give the Fawn shade to Drabs. Combined with alum, or Crystals of Tin, a fine Golden Yellow is obtained.

FUSTIC, OR YOUNG FUSTIC.—The best *Old Fustic* is imported from Cuba, and yields a permanent yellow coloring matter when combined with Alum and Argol, in dyeing various shades of Greens. See Receipts Nos. 12 and 13, Colored Merinoes; also used after Chroming for Olives of different shades; see Receipt No. 7, Orleans from Black Warps, &c. *Young Fustic* is chiefly used in dyeing Yellows, Oranges, and Scarlets. See Receipts from 8 to 11, Colored Orleans. It gives a bright Yellow when combined with Nitrate, Muriate, or Oxalic Tin, the last being the most effectual.

GALLS.—The Gall-nut is chiefly imported from Aleppo. It yields an astringent Black coloring matter, when combined with Copperas and Logwood; and it is generally employed in dyeing Silver Drabs upon Cotton, when combined with Nitrate of Iron. As a Dyeware, it gives greater solidity than Sumach for those light shades. *Volones* have nearly the same properties.

INDIGO.—It is produced from the leaves of *Indigofera,* a plant cultivated in South America, East Indies, &c. It is a very permanent coloring matter, employed in dyeing the majority of colors, varying from a Drab to an Indigo Blue. The color produced by it is often imitated by dyeing with Logwood, Worsteds and Woollens which have previously undergone the Chroming process. See Receipt No. 32, Worsted Yarn Dyeing.

KERMES, OR LAC DYE.—It is obtained from an insect deposited on different species of trees in the East Indies and other places. It contains red coloring matter, very like that of Cochineal, and is frequently used as a substitute for it, being thought by some Chemists to possess more permanence. It dyes good Scarlets, along with Nitrate of Tin, or Oxalic Tin, and Tartar. This Dye is much cheaper than Cochineal, and the difference of color is only slightly perceptible. See Receipts Nos. 10 and 11.

LOGWOOD.—This is a Dark Red Dyewood, and is much employed in dyeing Black upon Silk, Cotton, and Woollen; also for Blues and many other colors. Logwood, on first being introduced into England, was denounced by the cultivators of the native Woad, and even prohibited in England by Queen Elizabeth. All imported was to be destroyed; nor was it allowed to be used till the reign of Charles the Second.

MADDER.—This is obtained from the root of the *Rubia Tinctorum*, which grows wild in the South of Europe, &c. It is an article of great importance in dyeing. Madder possesses five distinct coloring principles, viz., madder red, madder purple, madder orange, madder yellow, and madder brown. These colors are of most use to Calico Printers. It is also used by Dyers to deaden Drabs; and with acid, &c., to dye many shades of Drabs. See Receipts Nos. 37 and 38, Colored Merinos.

NITRIC ACID, OR AQUA FORTIS.—This Spirit is much used in Dyeing. It is made from Nitrate of Potass, or Nitrate of Soda, and Sulphuric Acid. It will dye Silk yellow of itself, but is generally killed with Tin for Worsteds and Woollens.

NITRATES.—Nitrate of Tin is Aqua Fortis killed with Tin, which is used in dyeing Yellows, Buffs, Scarlets, and Crimsons, upon Worsted and Woollen Goods. See Receipt No. 47, Worsted Yarns. Nitrate of Iron is Aqua Fortis killed with Iron, or Copperas. It is used for dyeing Buffs upon Cotton, and as a mordant or preparation for other colors. Nitrate of Copper is Aqua Fortis killed with Copper, which is very useful for spending Catechu, combined with Sulphate of Copper.

OXALIC TIN.—This is a most valuable Spirit for dyeing all grain colors, brighter colors being obtained by it than by either Nitrate of Tin or Muriate of Tin. It is the best destroyer of Gum, sometimes found in Lac, and which is very injurious in dyeing. In Woollens it is very penetrating, dyeing the piece through, however strong, without leaving any white appearance. As yet, it is only partially known by the Dyers, but much approved by those who have tested its excellency.

PEACHWOOD.—This is used for dyeing Mock Crimsons, Maroons, and Clarets, upon Worsted, Woollen, and Cotton Goods, as may be seen from many of the Receipts in this book. It dyes very bright colors after a preparation of Alum, and darker shades of the same colors after a preparation of Chrome.

PRUSSIATE OF POTASS.—This is made from Pearlash and animal substances, as horns and hoofs; it is very extensively used by Dyers for dyeing Prussian Blues, varying from a Sky to a Royal Blue upon Cotton Fabrics. The *Bright Victoria Blue* is obtained from Prussiate as follows: First rinse the Yarns or Warps in a solution of Nitrate of Iron and a few Crystals of Tin; then rinse in a solution of Prussiate. The best mode, however, is by first rinsing in Muriate of Tin diluted with Water; then in a decoction of Logwood; after which, let them pass through the first process above described, with less Prussiate. This mode will produce a more bloomy color than that obtained by the first mode.

QUERCITRON BARK.—This is obtained from the Yellow Oak (*quercus negra*), growing in North America. It furnishes an excellent Yellow color. Alum and Muriate of Tin are the principal Mordants employed in dyeing Woollen and Cotton; but Oxalic Tin is the most efficient. It produces excellent Drabs upon Cotton with Nitrate of Iron.

SAFFLOWER.—The flowers of the *Carthamus Tinctorius*, grown chiefly in Spain, contain two coloring matters, yellow and red; the yellow is carried off by well washing in water until the flowers assume a bright crimson appearance; the red coloring matter is extracted by steeping in Pearlash and water, with occasional stirring; the liquor is then pressed from the flower, and is ready for dyeing Pink upon Cotton fabrics, combined with a little Tartaric or Sulphuric Acid. There is also a decoction of Safflower, which is sold in bottles. See Receipt No. 1, Shot Cobourgs.

SAUNDERS, OR RED SANDAL.—This is the wood of the *Pterocarpus santalinus*, grown in India. It possesses deep red coloring matter, and is used chiefly in dyeing Woollen Goods. It is more permanent than Peachwood, though not of so bright a color.

SAPAN WOOD.—This wood produces a red color, similar to that obtained from Peachwood, but it is not much used for dyeing purposes. It is generally sold in the Liquid state, and is used in Padding and Printing. See Receipt No. 2, Art of Padding.

SUMACH.—This astringent vegetable production is extensively used chiefly for Cotton dyeing. It is used as the base of many colors. The best is that imported from Sicily. It has great affinity for Iron, which, when combined with Sumach in certain proportions, imparts to Cotton a variety of shades from Silver Drab to Black.

TURMERIC.—This is the root of a plant cultivated in the East Indies, and contains much yellow coloring matter. It is frequently used instead of Fustic, but is not so permanent.

EXAMINATION OF WATER BY TESTS, OR REAGENTS.

TO ASCERTAIN IF WATER BE HARD OR SOFT.

Procure a small quantity of Soap dissolved in Alcohol, and let a few drops of it fall into a glass of the water to be tried. If the water becomes milky, it is hard; but if little or no milkiness takes place, the water may be said to be soft.

TO ASCERTAIN IF WATER CONTAIN AN ACID.

Take a piece of paper, containing no sizing, and which has been previously stained with Litmus, Syrup of Violets, or scrapings of Radishes, and immerse it in the water to be examined; if the paper becomes red, it contains an Acid. If a little limewater be added to the same water, and a precipitate takes place, it is Carbonic Acid. If dark blue paper, such as is wrapped round loaves of sugar, be converted to red, it contains a Mineral Acid.

TO ASCERTAIN IF WATER CONTAIN AN ALKALI OR AN EARTH.

Take a piece of paper which has been stained with an infusion of Litmus, and reddened by Vinegar, and immerse it in the water; if the blue color of the paper be restored, it either contains an alkali or an earth.

If a little of the Syrup of Violets be added to the water which contains an alkali or an earth, the water will become Green.

TO ASCERTAIN IF WATER CONTAIN IRON.

Take a glass of water and add to it a few drops of the infusion of Nutgalls, or suspend a Nutgall in it, by means of a thread, for 24 hours; if Iron be present, the water will become of a dark Brown or Black color.

Prussiate of Potash is a still more delicate test for detecting Iron. If a Crystal, or a drop of it when dissolved, be added to a glass of water containing Iron, it will immediately become of a Blue color.

TO ASCERTAIN IF WATER CONTAIN ANY SUBSTANCE COMBINED WITH MURIATIC ACID.

Take a glass of water and let a few drops of Nitrate of Silver fall into it; if a milkiness be produced, which disappears on the addition of a little Liquid Ammonia, it may be concluded that some salt with Muriatic Acid is present. Muriate of Lime, Muriate of Soda (common salt), and Muriate of Magnesia are the salts most generally to be met with in spring water.

TO ASCERTAIN IF WATER CONTAIN MAGNESIA.

Take a quantity of the water, and boil down to a twentieth part of its bulk, then drop a few grains of Carbonate of Ammonia into a small glass of water. No Magnesia will yet be precipitated; but on adding a small quantity of Phosphate of Soda, if any Magnesia be present, it will then make its appearance, and fall to the bottom of the glass. Observation.—In this experiment, it is necessary that the Carbonate of Ammonia be in a neutral state.

TO ASCERTAIN IF WATER CONTAIN PURE LIME.

Into a glass of the water drop a Crystal or two of Oxalic Acid; if a precipitate takes place, and if another glass of the same water becomes milky upon blowing air from the lungs into it through a quill, the presence of pure Lime, or Barytes, may be inferred; but Barytes has never yet been found pure in water.

TO ASCERTAIN IF WATER CONTAIN CARBONIC ACID.

Take a quantity of the water, and add to it an equal quantity of perfectly transparent limewater. If Carbonic Acid be present, either free or combined, a precipitate immediately appears, which on adding a few drops of Muriatic Acid will again be dissolved with effervescence.

TO ASCERTAIN IF WATER CONTAIN ANY COMBINATION OF SULPHUR.

Put a little Quicksilver into a phial of water, cork it, and let it stand for a few hours. If the surface of the quicksilver has acquired a black appearance, and a blackish powder separates from it on shaking the phial, the presence of Sulphur may be inferred.

TO ASCERTAIN IF WATER CONTAIN LEAD.

To a little of the water in a glass add an equal portion of water impregnated with Sulphuretted Gas. If Lead be present, it will be known by the color of the water, which will assume a dark Brown or blackish tinge. Observation.—Lead may be also detected by adding a little Sulphuret of Ammonia or Potash. A similar effect will take place as in the last experiment, if Lead be present.

TO ASCERTAIN IF WATER CONTAIN COPPER.

Immerse a polished plate of Iron in the water to be examined, and let it remain in a few minutes. If Copper be present, the plate of Iron will be coated over with Copper. Observation.—A few drops of Liquid Ammonia will turn any water containing Copper to a deep blue color.

EXPLANATION OF TERMS, ETC,

A *Tot* is equal to about ⅛ of a Pint.

A *Pailful* will amount to about 3 or 4 Gallons.

Dishful. Instead of using this term, 10 lbs. has been substituted in the course of this work.

Where it is said *Worsted dye*, with a certain quantity of wares, it means that the Worsted must be dyed before the Cotton, and the Cotton afterwards.

When it is said *Sumach*, it means that the Pieces must be run in Sumach Liquor prepared in the following manner: Boil up about 100 lbs. in the bottom of a Cistern, stir it up well for about 15 minutes, and then add sufficient cold water; this will be about sufficient for 80 Pieces; the first 40 to be turned on about half an hour, the latter to be turned on about an hour, or to be steeped in the liquor for the same length of time. After about 80 Pieces have been prepared, the liquor will still retain some strength, and by adding a little more Sumach, either boiled or dry, the Liquor will then prepare 80 Pieces more, by being steeped in it all night, and draining out all the strength. Less Sumach will be required when a considerable quantity of Pieces are prepared, but not less than 2 lbs. to a Piece will prepare 10 at once. But where a Sumach Vessel is continually used, the better way is to boil up a quantity of Sumach at once in a separate vessel, and replenish as occasion may require. Some Dyers prefer a mere infusion of Sumach in cold Water.

When it is said *Iron*, it means to run the Pieces in diluted Nitrate of Iron. When a vessel is first used, a little more Iron is required than is stated in some of the Receipts for White

29

Warped Orleans and Cobourgs; but no more than is stated after the vessel is seasoned; for the more iron is used, the Blacker appearance the Pieces will have. Where the least Iron can be used, the clearer the Pieces will appear. It is not advisable to work the same Liquor more than a few days, wherever Sumached Pieces are being continually run in it, for it frequently precipitates the Iron and Sumach together, forming a sort of a paste of a blubber appearance, which leaves streaks and stains in the Pieces which cannot be seen in the Ironed state. I have had Pieces dryed after being Ironed, to prove how the stains were produced, and I have found them to have been produced in the Ironing process. Some Dyers, not properly understanding the nature of the article, use pailful after pailful of Nitrate of Iron, where one-fourth of the quantity would do much better. It has a great affinity for Sumach, and as soon as it comes in contact with it, it produces a dark slate or thin black color; by adding a portion of Logwood, a Black is formed. Sometimes the Nitrate of Iron may not be sufficiently killed, or has not sufficient Iron in it. When this is the case, it will destroy the Sumach, and leave the Cotton a thin Drab, instead of a thin Black, and it will not take Logwood for Black; and if the warp be for a Brown or Claret, the Piece has to be Cotton-dyed again; the effect of which is seldom seen until the Pieces are dyed, which, if Cotton-dyed in this manner, are never so handsome.

To *Spirit*, means to run, or prepare, say 10 Pieces, in about 1 Quart of Muriate of Tin, diluted with water, in a Cistern which will hold the Pieces conveniently, and turned on about 8 ends: 20 or 30 Pieces may be spirited by adding half a Pint more Spirits. Some Dyers prefer Spiriting and Ironing in Troughs made for the purpose, and this plan is certainly more expeditious, and does not require so much Spirit.

PUBLICATIONS

OF

HENRY CAREY BAIRD,

SUCCESSOR TO E. L. CAREY,

No. 7 Hart's Building, Sixth Street above Chestnut, Philadelphia.

SCIENTIFIC AND PRACTICAL.

THE PRACTICAL MODEL CALCULATOR,

FOR the Engineer, Machinist, Manufacturer of Engine Work, Naval Architect, Miner, and Millwright. By OLIVER BYRNE, Compiler and Editor of the Dictionary of Machines, Mechanics, Engine Work and Engineering, and Author of various Mathematical and Mechanical Works. Illustrated by numerous Engravings. Now Complete, One large Volume, Octavo, of nearly six hundred pages..$3.50

It will contain such calculations as are met with and required in the Mechanical Arts, and establish models or standards to guide practical men. The Tables that are introduced, many of which are new, will greatly economize labour, and render the every-day calculations of the *practical man* comprehensive and easy. From every single calculation given in this work numerous other calculations are readily modelled, so that each may be considered the head of a numerous family of practical results.

The examples selected will be found appropriate, and in all cases taken from the actual practice of the present time. Every rule has been tested by the unerring results of mathematical research, and confirmed by experiment, when such was necessary.

The Practical Model Calculator will be found to fill a vacancy in the library of the practical working-man long considered a requirement. It will be found to excel all other works of a similar nature, from the great extent of its range, the exemplary nature of its well-selected examples, and from the easy, simple, and systematic manner in which the model calculations are established.

NORRIS'S HAND-BOOK FOR LOCOMOTIVE ENGINEERS AND MACHINISTS:

Comprising the Calculations for Constructing Locomotives Manner of setting Valves, &c. &c. By SEPTIMUS NORRIS, Civil and Mechanical Engineer. In One Volume, 12mo., with illustrations.. $1.50

With pleasure do we meet with such a work as Messrs. Norris and Baird have given us.—*Artisan.*

In this work, he has given what are called the "secrets of the business," in the rules to construct locomotives, in order that the million should be learned in all things.—*Scientific American.*

THE ARTS OF TANNING AND CURRYING

Theoretically and Practically considered in all their details. Being a full and comprehensive Treatise on the Manufacture of the various kinds of Leather. Illustrated by over two hundred Engravings. Edited from the French of De Fontenelle and Malapeyere. With numerous Emendations and Additions, by CAMPBELL MORFIT, Practical and Analytical Chemist. Complete in one Volume, octavo..$5.00

This important Treatise will be found to cover the whole field in the most masterly manner, and it is believed that in no other branch of applied science could more signal service be rendered to American Manufacturers.

The publisher is not aware that in any other work heretofore issued in this country, more space has been devoted to this subject than a single chapter; and in offering this volume to so large and intelligent a class as American Tanners and Leather Dressers, he feels confident of their substantial support and encouragement.

———

THE PRACTICAL COTTON-SPINNER AND MANUFACTURER; Or, The Manager's and Overseer's Companion.

This works contains a Comprehensive System of Calculations for Mill Gearing and Machinery, from the first moving power through the different processes of Carding, Drawing, Slabbing, Roving, Spinning, and Weaving, adapted to American Machinery, Practice, and Usages. Compendious Tables of Yarns and Reeds are added. Illustrated by large Working-drawings of the most approved American Cotton Machinery. Complete in One Volume, octavo.. ....$3.50

This edition of Scott's Cotton-Spinner, by OLIVER BYRNE, is designed for the American Operative. It will be found intensely practical, and will be of the greatest possible value to the Manager, Overseer, and Workman.

———

THE PRACTICAL METAL-WORKER'S ASSISTANT,

For Tin-Plate Workers, Brasiers, Coppersmiths, Zinc-Plate Ornamenters and Workers, Wire Workers, Whitesmiths, Blacksmiths, Bell Hangers, Jewellers, Silver and Gold Smiths, Electrotypers, and all other Workers in Alloys and Metals. By CHARLES HOLTZAPPFEL. Edited, with important additions, by OLIVER BYRNE. Complete in One Volume, octavo............$4.00

It will treat of Casting, Founding, and Forging; of Tongs and other Tools; Degrees of Heat and Managemnet of Fires; Welding; of Heading and Swage Tools; of Punches and Anvils; of Hardening and Tempering; of Malleable Iron Castings, Case Hardening, Wrought and Cast Iron. The management and manipulation of Metals and Alloys, Melting and Mixing. The management of Furnaces, Casting and Founding with Metallic Moulds, Joining and Working Sheet Metal. Peculiarities of the different Tools employed. Processes dependent on the ductility of Metals. Wire Drawing, Drawing Metal Tubes, Soldering. The use of the Blowpipe, and every other known Metal-Worker's Tool. To the works of Holtzappfel, OLIVER BYRNE has added all that is useful and peculiar to the American Metal-Worker.

THE MANUFACTURE OF IRON IN ALL ITS VARIOUS BRANCHES:

To which is added an Essay on the Manufacture of Steel, by FREDERICK OVERMAN, Mining Engineer, with one hundred and fifty Wood Engravings. A new edition. In One Volume, octavo, five hundred pages...$5.00

We have now to announce the appearance of another valuable work on the subject which, in our humble opinion, supplies any deficiency which late improvements and discoveries may have caused, from the lapse of time since the date of "Mushet" and "Schrivenor." It is the production of one of our transatlantic brethren, Mr. Frederick Overman, Mining Engineer; and we do not hesitate to set it down as a work of great importance to all connected with the iron interest; one which, while it is sufficiently technological fully to explain chemical analysis, and the various phenomena of iron under different circumstances, to the satisfaction of the most fastidious, is written in that clear and comprehensive style as to be available to the capacity of the humblest mind, and consequently will be of much advantage to those works where the proprietors may see the desirability of placing it in the hands of their operatives.— *London Morning Journal.*

A TREATISE ON THE AMERICAN STEAM-ENGINE.

Illustrated by numerous Wood Cuts and other Engravings. By OLIVER BYRNE. In One Volume.   (In press.)

PROPELLERS AND STEAM NAVIGATION:

With Biographical Sketches of Early Inventors. By ROBERT MACFARLANE, C. E., Editor of the "Scientific American." In One Volume, 12mo. Illustrated by over Eighty Wood Engravings ....75 cts.

The object of this "History of Propellers and Steam Navigation" is twofold. One is the arrangement and description of many devices which have been invented to propel vessels, in order to prevent many ingenious men from wasting their time, talents, and money on such projects. The immense amount of time, study, and money thrown away on such contrivances is beyond calculation. In this respect, it is hoped that it will be the means of doing some good.— *Preface.*

A TREATISE ON SCREW-PROPELLERS AND THEIR STEAM-ENGINES.

With Practical Rules and Examples by which to Calculate and Construct the same for any description of Vessels. By J. W. NYSTROM. Illustrated by thirty-two large working Drawings. In one Volume, octavo...$3.50

PRACTICAL SERIES.

THE AMERICAN MILLER AND MILLWRIGHT'S ASSIST-
ANT. $1.
THE TURNER'S COMPANION. 75 cts.
THE PAINTER, GILDER, AND VARNISHER'S COMPA-
NION. 75 cts.
THE DYER AND COLOUR-MAKER'S COMPANION. 75 cts.
THE BUILDER'S COMPANION. $1.
THE CABINET-MAKER'S COMPANION. 75 cts.
A TREATISE ON A BOX OF INSTRUMENTS. BY THOMAS
KENTISH. $1.
THE PAPER-HANGER'S COMPANION. BY J. ARROWSMITH.
75 cts.
THE ASSAYER'S GUIDE. BY OSCAR M. LIEBER. 75 cts.
THE COMPLETE PRACTICAL BREWER. BY M. L. BYRN. $1.
THE COMPLETE PRACTICAL DISTILLER. BY M. L. BYRN. $1.
THE BOOKBINDER'S MANUAL.
THE PYROTECHNIST'S COMPANION. BY G. W. MORTI-
MER. 75 cts.
WALKER'S ELECTROTYPE MANIPULATION. 75 cts.
COLBURN ON THE LOCOMOTIVE ENGINE. 75 cts.

THE AMERICAN MILLER AND MILLWRIGHT'S ASSISTANT:

By WILLIAM CARTER HUGHES, Editor of "The American Miller," (newspaper,) Buffalo, N. Y. Illustrated by Drawings of
the most approved Machinery. In One Volume, 12mo........$1

The author offers it as a substantial reference, instead of speculative theories,
which belong only to those not immediately attached to the business. Special
notice is also given of most of the essential improvements which have of late
been introduced for the benefit of the Miller.—*Savannah Republican.*
The whole business of making flour is most thoroughly treated by him.—
Bulletin
A very comprehensive view of the Millwright's business.—*Southern Literary
Messenger.*

THE TURNER'S COMPANION:

Containing Instructions in Concentric, Elliptic, and Eccentric
Turning. Also, various Plates of Chucks, Tools, and Instru-
ments, and Directions for using the Eccentric Cutter, Drill,
Vertical Cutter, and Circular Rest; with Patterns and Instruc-
tions for working them. Illustrated by numerous Engravings.
In One Volume, 12mo...75 cts.

The object of the Turner's Companion is to explain in a clear, concise, and
intelligible manner, the rudiments of this beautiful art.—*Savannah Republican.*
There is no description of turning or lathe-work that this elegant little treatise
does not describe and illustrate —*Western Lit. Messenger.*

THE PAINTER, GILDER, AND VARNISHER'S COMPANION:

Containing Rules and Regulations for every thing relating to the arts of Painting, Gilding, Varnishing, and Glass Staining: numerous useful and valuable Receipts; Tests for the detection of Adulterations in Oils, Colours, &c., and a Statement of the Diseases and Accidents to which Painters, Gilders, and Varnishers are particularly liable; with the simplest methods of Prevention and Remedy. In one vol. small 12mo., cloth. 75cts.

Rejecting all that appeared foreign to the subject, the compiler has omitted nothing of real practical worth.—*Hunt's Merchant's Magazine.*

An excellent *practical work*, and one which the practical man cannot afford to be without.—*Farmer and Mechanic.*

It contains every thing that is of interest to persons engaged in this trade. —*Bulletin.*

This book will prove valuable to all whose business is in any way connected with painting.—*Scott's Weekly.*

Cannot fail to be useful.—*N. Y. Commercial.*

THE BUILDER'S POCKET COMPANION:

Containing the Elements of Building, Surveying, and Architecture; with Practical Rules and Instructions connected with the subject. By A. C. SMEATON, Civil Engineer, &c. In one volume, 12mo. $1.

CONTENTS:—The Builder, Carpenter, Joiner, Mason, Plasterer, Plumber, Painter, Smith, Practical Geometry, Surveyor, Cohesive Strength of Bodies, Architect.

It gives, in a small space, the most thorough directions to the builder, from the laying of a brick, or the felling of a tree, up to the most elaborate production of ornamental architecture. It is scientific, without being obscure and unintelligible, and every house-carpenter, master, journeyman, or apprentice, should have a copy at hand always.—*Evening Bulletin.*

Complete on the subjects of which it treats. A most useful practical work. —*Balt. American.*

It must be of great practical utility.—*Savannah Republican.*

To whatever branch of the art of building the reader may belong, he will find in this something valuable and calculated to assist his progress.—*Farmer and Mechanic.*

This is a valuable little volume, designed to assist the student in the acquisition of elementary knowledge, and will be found highly advantageous to every young man who has devoted himself to the interesting pursuits of which it treats.—*Va. Herald.*

1*

THE DYER AND COLOUR-MAKER'S COMPANION:

Containing upwards of two hundred Receipts for making Colors, on the most approved principles, for all the various styles and fabrics now in existence; with the Scouring Process, and plain Directions for Preparing, Washing-off, and Finishing the Goods. In one volume, small 12mo., cloth. 75 cts.

This is another of that most excellent class of practical books, which the publisher is giving to the public. Indeed we believe there is not, for manufacturers, a more valuable work, having been prepared for, and expressly adapted to their business.—*Farmer and Mechanic.*

It is a valuable book.—*Otsego Republican.*

We have shown it to some practical men, who all pronounced it the completest thing of the kind they had seen—*N. Y. Nation.*

THE CABINET-MAKER AND UPHOLSTERER'S COMPANION:

Comprising the Rudiments and Principles of Cabinet Making and Upholstery, with familiar instructions, illustrated by Examples, for attaining a proficiency in the Art of Drawing, as applicable to Cabinet Work; the processes of Veneering, Inlaying, and Buhl Work; the art of Dyeing and Staining Wood, Ivory, Bone, Tortoise-shell, etc. Directions for Lackering, Japanning, and Varnishing; to make French Polish; to prepare the best Glues, Cements, and Compositions, and a number of Receipts particularly useful for Workmen generally, with Explanatory and Illustrative Engravings. By J. Stokes. In one volume, 12mo., with illustrations. Second Edition. 75 cts.

THE PAPER-HANGER'S COMPANION:

In which the Practical Operations of the Trade are systematically laid down; with copious Directions Preparatory to Papering; Preventions against the effect of Damp in Walls; the various Cements and Pastes adapted to the several purposes of the Trade; Observations and Directions for the Panelling and Ornamenting of Rooms, &c. &c. By James Arrowsmith. In One Volume, 12mo. 75 cts.

THE ANALYTICAL CHEMIST'S ASSISTANT:

A Manual of Chemical Analysis, both Qualitative and Quantitative, of Natural and Artificial Inorganic Compounds; to which are appended the Rules for Detecting Arsenic in a Case of Poisoning. By FREDERIK WŒHLER, Professor of Chemistry in the University of Göttingen. Translated from the German, with an Introduction, Illustrations, and copious Additions, by OSCAR M. LIEBER, Author of the "Assayer's Guide." In one Volume, 12mo. $1.25.

RURAL CHEMISTRY:

An Elementary Introduction to the Study of the Science, in its relation to Agriculture and the Arts of Life. By EDWARD SOLLEY, Professor of Chemistry in the Horticultural Society of London. From the Third Improved London Edition. 12mo. $1.25.

THE FRUIT, FLOWER, AND KITCHEN GARDEN.

By PATRICK NEILL, L.L.D.

Thoroughly revised, and adapted to the climate and seasons of the United States, by a Practical Horticulturist. Illustrated by numerous Engravings. In one volume, 12mo. $1.25.

HOUSEHOLD SURGERY; OR, HINTS ON EMERGENCIES.

By J. F. SOUTH, one of the Surgeons of St. Thomas's Hospital. In one volume, 12mo. Illustrated by nearly fifty Engravings. $1.25.

HOUSEHOLD MEDICINE.

In one volume, 12mo. Uniform with, and a companion to, the above. (In immediate preparation.)

THE COMPLETE PRACTICAL BREWER;

Or, Plain, Concise, and Accurate Instructions in the Art of Brewing Beer, Ale, Porter, &c. &c., and the Process of Making all the Small Beers. By M. LAFAYETTE BYRN, M. D. With Illustrations, 12mo. $1.

THE COMPLETE PRACTICAL DISTILLER;

By M. LAFAYETTE BYRN, M. D. With Illustrations, 12mo. $1.

THE ENCYCLOPEDIA OF CHEMISTRY, PRACTI-CAL AND THEORETICAL:

Embracing its application to the Arts, Metallurgy, Mineralogy, Geology, Medicine, and Pharmacy. By JAMES C. BOOTH, Melter and Refiner in the United States Mint; Professor of Applied Chemistry in the Franklin Institute, etc.; assisted by CAMPBELL MORFIT, author of "Chemical Manipulations," etc. Complete in one volume, royal octavo, 978 pages, with numerous wood cuts and other illustrations. $5.

It covers the whole field of Chemistry as applied to Arts and Sciences. * * * As no library is complete without a common dictionary, it is also our opinion that none can be without this Encyclopedia of Chemistry.—*Scientific American.*

A work of time and labour, and a treasury of chemical information.—*North American.*

By far the best manual of the kind which has been presented to the American public.—*Boston Courier.*

PERFUMERY; ITS MANUFACTURE AND USE:

With Instructions in every branch of the Art, and Receipts for all the Fashionable Preparations; the whole forming a valuable aid to the Perfumer, Druggist, and Soap Manufacturer. Illustrated by numerous Wood-cuts. From the French of Celnart, and other late authorities. With Additions and Improvements by CAMPBELL MORFIT, one of the Editors of the "Encyclopedia of Chemistry." In one volume, 12mo., cloth. $1.50

A TREATISE ON A BOX OF INSTRUMENTS,

And the SLIDE RULE, with the Theory of Trigonometry and Logarithms, including Practical Geometry, Surveying, Measuring of Timber, Cask and Malt Gauging, Heights and Distances. By THOMAS KENTISH. In One Volume, 12mo. $1.

THE LOCOMOTIVE ENGINE:

Including a Description of its Structure, Rules for Estimating its Capabilities, and Practical Observations on its Construction and Management. By ZERAH COLBURN, 12mo..............75 cts.

SYLLABUS OF A COMPLETE COURSE OF LECTURES ON CHEMISTRY:

Including its Application to the Arts, Agriculture, and Mining, prepared for the use of the Gentlemen Cadets at the Hon. E. I. Co.'s Military Seminary, Addiscombe. By Professor E. SOLLY, Lecturer on Chemistry in the Hon. E. I. Co.'s Military Seminary. Revised by the Author of "Chemical Manipulations." In one volume, octavo, cloth. $1.25.

THE ASSAYER'S GUIDE;

Or, Practical Directions to Assayers, Miners, and Smelters, for the Tests and Assays, by Heat and by Wet Processes, of the Ores of all the principal Metals, and of Gold and Silver Coins and Alloys. By OSCAR M. LIEBER, late Geologist to the State of Mississippi. 12mo. With Illustrations. 75 cts.

THE BOOKBINDER'S MANUAL.

Complete in one Volume, 12mo. (in press.)

ELECTROTYPE MANIPULATION:

Being the Theory and Plain Instructions in the Art of Working
in Metals, by Precipitating them from their Solutions, through
the agency of Galvanic or Voltaic Electricity. By CHARLES V.
WALKER, Hon. Secretary to the London Electrical Society, etc
Illustrated by Wood-cuts. A New Edition, from the Twenty-
fifth London Edition. 12mo. 75 cts.

PHOTOGENIC MANIPULATION:

Containing the Theory and Plain Instructions in the Art of
Photography, or the Productions of Pictures through the Agency
of Light; including Calotype, Chrysotype, Cyanotype, Chroma-
type, Energiatype, Anthotype, Amphitype, Daguerreotype,
Thermography, Electrical and Galvanic Impressions. By
GEORGE THOMAS FISHER, Jr., Assistant in the Laboratory of
the London Institution. Illustrated by wood-cuts. In one volume, 24mo., cloth. 62 cts.

MATHEMATICS FOR PRACTICAL MEN:

Being a Common-Place Book of Principles, Theorems, Rules,
and Tables, in various departments of Pure and Mixed Mathe-
matics, with their Applications; especially to the pursuits of
Surveyors, Architects, Mechanics, and Civil Engineers, with numerous Engravings. By OLINTHUS GREGORY, L.L.D. $1.50.

Only let men awake, and fix their eyes, one while on the nature of things,
another while on the application of them to the use and service of mankind.
—*Lord Bacon.*

EXAMINATIONS OF DRUGS, MEDICINES, CHE-
MICALS, &c.

As to their Purity and Adulterations. By C. H. PEIRCE, M.D.,
Translator of "Stöckhardt's Chemistry," Examiner of Medicines
for the Port of Boston, &c. &c. 12mo, cloth...............$1.25

SHEEP-HUSBANDRY IN THE SOUTH:

Comprising a Treatise on the Acclimation of Sheep in the Southern States, and an Account of the different Breeds. Also, a Complete Manual of Breeding, Summer and Winter Management, and of the Treatment of Diseases. With Portraits and other Illustrations. By HENRY S. RANDALL. In One Volume, octavo........ ....$1.25

ELWOOD'S GRAIN TABLES:

Showing the value of Bushels and Pounds of different kinds of Grain, calculated in Federal Money, so arranged as to exhibit upon a single page the value at a given price from *ten cents to two dollars* per bushel, of any quantity from *one pound to ten thousand bushels.* By J. L. ELWOOD. A new Edition. In One Volume, 12mo........ .... $1

To Millers and Produce Dealers this work is pronounced by all who have it in use, to be superior in arrangement to any work of the kind published—and *unerring accuracy in every calculation may be relied upon in every instance.*
☞ A reward of Twenty-five Dollars is offered for an error of one cent found in the work.

MISS LESLIE'S COMPLETE COOKERY.

Directions for Cookery, in its Various Branches. By MISS LESLIE. Forty-seventh Edition. Thoroughly Revised, with the Addition of New Receipts. In One Volume, 12mo, half bound, or in sheep........ ....$1

In preparing a new and carefully revised edition of this my first work on cookery, I have introduced improvements, corrected errors, and added new receipts, that I trust will on trial be found satisfactory. The success of the book (proved by its immense and increasing circulation) affords conclusive evidence that it has obtained the approbation of a large number of my countrywomen; many of whom have informed me that it has made practical housewives of young ladies who have entered into married life with no other acquirements than a few showy accomplishments. Gentlemen, also, have told me of great improvements in the family table, after presenting their wives with this manual of domestic cookery, and that, after a morning devoted to the fatigues of business, they no longer find themselves subjected to the annoyance of an ill-dressed dinner.—*Preface.*

MISS LESLIE'S TWO HUNDRED RECEIPTS IN FRENCH COOKERY.

A new Edition, in cloth...25 cts.

THE DYER'S INSTRUCTOR,

Comprising Practical Instructions in the Art of Dyeing Silk, Cotton, Wool and Worsted and Woollen Goods, &c., containing nearly 800 Receipts, to which is added the Art of Padding and the Printing of Silk Warps, Skeins, and Handkerchiefs, and the various Mordants and Colours for the different styles of such work. By DAVID SMITH, Pattern Dyer, 1 vol. 12mo, (just published) $1.50

TWO HUNDRED DESIGNS FOR COTTAGES AND VILLAS, &c. &c.

Original and Selected. By THOMAS U. WALTER, Architect of Girard College, and JOHN JAY SMITH, Librarian of the Philadelphia Library. In Four Parts, quarto..............................$10

GUIDE FOR WORKERS IN METALS AND STONE.

Consisting of Designs and Patterns for Gates, Piers, Balcony and Cemetery Railing, Window Guards, Balustrades, Staircases, Verandas, Fanlights, Lamps and Lamp Posts, Palisades, Monuments, Mantles, Gas Fittings, Stoves, Stands, Candlesticks, Silver and Plated Ware, Chandeliers, Candelabras, Potters' Ware, &c. &c. By T. U. WALTER, Architect, and JOHN JAY SMITH, 4 vols. 4to, plates. $10

FAMILY ENCYCLOPEDIA

Of Useful Knowledge and General Literature; containing about Four Thousand Articles upon Scientific and Popular Subjects. With Plates. By JOHN L. BLAKE, D. D. In One Volume, 8vo, cloth extra..$3.50

THE PYROTECHNIST'S COMPANION;

Or, A Familiar System of Recreative Fire-Works. By G. W. MORTIMER. Illustrated by numerous Engravings. 12mo. 75 cts

STANDARD ILLUSTRATED POETRY.

THE TALES AND POEMS OF LORD BYRON:

Illustrated by Henry Warren. In One Volume, royal 8vo.
with 10 Plates, scarlet cloth, gilt edges...............................$5
Morocco extra..$7

It is illustrated by several elegant engravings, from original designs by Warren, and is a most splendid work for the parlour or study.—*Boston Evening Gazette.*

CHILDE HAROLD; A ROMAUNT BY LORD BYRON:

Illustrated by 12 Splendid Plates, by Warren and others. In
One Volume, royal 8vo., cloth extra, gilt edges...................$5
Morocco extra $7

Printed in elegant style, with splendid pictures, far superior to any thing of the sort usually found in books of this kind.—*N. Y. Courier.*

THE FEMALE POETS OF AMERICA.

By Rufus W. Griswold. A new Edition. In One Volume,
royal 8vo. Cloth, gilt..$2.50
Cloth extra, gilt edges...$3
Morocco super extra $4.50

The best production which has yet come from the pen of Dr. Griswold, and the most valuable contribution which he has ever made to the literary celebrity of the country.—*N. Y. Tribune.*

THE LADY OF THE LAKE:

By Sir Walter Scott. Illustrated with 10 Plates, by Corbould and Meadows. In One Volume, royal 8vo. Bound in
cloth extra, gilt edges...$5
Turkey morocco super extra...$7

This is one of the most truly beautiful books which has ever issued from the American press.

LALLA ROOKH; A ROMANCE BY THOMAS MOORE:

Illustrated by 13 Plates, from Designs by Corbould, Meadows, and Stephanoff. In One Volume, royal 8vo. Bound in
cloth extra, gilt edges..$5
Turkey morocco super extra..$7

This is published in a style uniform with the "Lady of the Lake."

THE POETICAL WORKS OF THOMAS GRAY:

With Illustrations by C. W. RADCLIFF. Edited with a Memoir, by HENRY REED, Professor of English Literature in the University of Pennsylvania. In One Volume, 8vo. Bound in cloth extra, gilt edges...$3.50
Turkey morocco super extra..$5.50
In One Volume, 12mo, without plates, cloth....................$1.25
Do.   do.   do.   cloth, gilt edges....$1.50

We have not seen a specimen of typographical luxury from the American press which can surpass this volume in choice elegance.—*Boston Courier.*
It is eminently calculated to consecrate among American readers, (if they have not been consecrated already in their hearts,) the pure, the elegant, the refined, and, in many respects, the sublime imaginings of THOMAS GRAY.—*Richmond Whig.*

THE POETICAL WORKS OF HENRY WADSWORTH LONGFELLOW:

Illustrated by 10 Plates, after Designs by D. HUNTINGDON, with a Portrait. Ninth Edition. In One Volume, royal 8vo. Bound in cloth extra, gilt edges...$5
Morocco super extra..$7

This is the very luxury of literature—LONGFELLOW's charming poems presented in a form of unsurpassed beauty.—*Neal's Gazette.*

POETS AND POETRY OF ENGLAND IN THE NINE-TEENTH CENTURY.

By RUFUS W. GRISWOLD. Illustrated. In One Volume, royal 8vo. Bound in cloth...$3
Cloth extra, gilt edges...$3.50
Morocco super extra..$5

Such is the critical acumen discovered in these selections, that scarcely a page is to be found but is redolent with beauties, and the volume itself may be regarded as a galaxy of literary pearls.—*Democratic Review.*

THE TASK, AND OTHER POEMS.

By WILLIAM COWPER. Illustrated by 10 Steel Engravings. In One Volume, 12mo. Cloth extra, gilt edges...................$2
Morocco extra..$3
"The illustrations in this edition of Cowper are most exquisitely designed and engraved."

THE FEMALE POETS OF GREAT BRITAIN.

With Copious Selections and Critical Remarks. By FREDERIC
ROWTON. With Additions. Illustrations. 8vo, cloth......$2.50
Cloth extra, gilt edges...$3.00
Turkey morocco, super...$4.50

Mr. ROWTON has presented us with admirably selected specimens of nearly
one hundred of the most celebrated female poets of Great Britain, from the
time of Lady Juliana Bernes, the first of whom there is any record, to the
Mitfords, the Hewitts, the Cooks, the Barretts, and others of the present day.—
Hunt's Merchants' Magazine.

SPECIMENS OF THE BRITISH POETS.

From the time of Chaucer to the end of the Eighteenth Century. By THOMAS CAMPBELL. In One Volume, royal 8vo.
(In press.)

THE POETS AND POETRY OF THE ANCIENTS:

By WILLIAM PETER, A. M. Comprising Translations and
Specimens of the Poets of Greece and Rome, with an elegant
engraved View of the Coliseum at Rome. Bound in cloth......$3
Cloth extra, gilt edges..$3.50
Turkey morocco super extra.....................................$5

It is without fear that we say that no such excellent or complete collection
has ever been made. It is made with skill, taste, and judgment.—*Charleston
Patriot.*

THE POETICAL WORKS OF N. PARKER WILLIS.

Illustrated by 16 Plates, after designs by E. LEUTZE. In One
Volume, royal 8vo. A new Edition. Bound in cloth extra,
gilt edges...$5
Turkey morocco super extra $7

This is one of the most beautiful works ever published in this country.—
Courier and Inquirer.

Pure and perfect in sentiment, often in expression, and many a heart has
been won from sorrow or roused from apathy by his earlier melodies. The
illustrations are by LEUTZE,—a sufficient guarantee for their beauty and grace.
As for the typographical execution of the volume, it will bear comparison with
any English book, and quite surpasses most issues in America.—*Neal's Gazette.*

The admirers of the poet could not have his gems in a better form for holi
day presents.— *W. Continent.*

MISCELLANEOUS.

JOURNAL OF ARNOLD'S EXPEDITION TO QUEBEC, IN 1775.

By ISAAC SENTER, M. D. 8vo, boards...............................62 cts.

ADVENTURES OF CAPTAIN SIMON SUGGS;

And other Sketches. By JOHNSON J. HOOPER. With Illustrations. 12mo, paper...50 cts.
Cloth...75 cts.

AUNT PATTY'S SCRAP-BAG.

By Mrs. CAROLINE LEE HENTZ, Author of "Linda." 12mo.
Paper covers...50 cts.
Cloth...75 cts.

BIG BEAR OF ARKANSAS;

And other Western Sketches. Edited by W. T. PORTER. In One Volume, 12mo, paper..50 cts.
Cloth...75 cts.

COMIC BLACKSTONE.

By GILBERT ABBOT A' BECKET. Illustrated. Complete in One Volume. Cloth...75 cts.

GHOST STORIES.

Illustrated by Designs by DARLEY. In One Volume, 12mo, paper covers...50 cts.

MODERN CHIVALRY; OR, THE ADVENTURES OF CAPTAIN FARRAGO AND TEAGUE O'REGAN.

By H. H. BRACKENRIDGE. Second Edition since the Author's death. With a Biographical Notice, a Critical Disquisition on the Work, and Explanatory Notes. With Illustrations, from Original Designs by DARLEY. Two volumes, paper covers 75cts.
Cloth or sheep...$1.00

COMPLETE WORKS OF LORD BOLINGBROKE·

With a Life, prepared expressly for this Edition, containing Additional Information relative to his Personal and Public Character, selected from the best authorities. In Four Volumes, 8vo. Bound in cloth...$7.00
In sheep...8.00

CHRONICLES OF PINEVILLE.

By the Author of "Major Jones's Courtship." Illustrated by DARLEY. 12mo, paper...50 cts.
Cloth ....75 cts.

GILBERT GURNEY.

By THEODORE HOOK. With Illustrations. In One Volume, 8vo., paper...50 cts.

MEMOIRS OF THE GENERALS, COMMODORES, AND OTHER COMMANDERS,

Who distinguished themselves in the American Army and Navy, during the War of the Revolution, the War with France, that with Tripoli, and the War of 1812, and who were presented with Medals, by Congress, for their gallant services. By THOMAS WYATT, A. M., Author of "History of the Kings of France." Illustrated with Eighty-two Engravings from the Medals. 8vo. Cloth gilt $2.00
Half morocco..$2.50

GEMS OF THE BRITISH POETS.

By S. C. HALL. In One Volume, 12mo., cloth............$1.00
Cloth, gilt $1.25

VISITS TO REMARKABLE PLACES:

Old Halls, Battle Fields, and Scenes Illustrative of striking passages in English History and Poetry. By WILLIAM HOWITT. In Two Volumes, 8vo, cloth.......................................$4.00

2*

NARRATIVE OF THE ARCTIC LAND EXPEDITION.

By CAPTAIN BACK, R. N. In One Volume, 8vo, boards...$2.00

THE MISCELLANEOUS WORKS OF WILLIAM HAZLITT.

Including Table-talk; Opinions of Books, Men, and Things; Lectures on Dramatic Literature of the Age of Elizabeth; Lectures on the English Comic Writers; The Spirit of the Age, or Contemporary Portraits. Five Volumes, 12mo., cloth......$5.00
Half calf..$6.25

FLORAL OFFERING

A Token of Friendship. Edited by FRANCES S. OSGOOD. Illustrated by 10 beautiful Bouquets of Flowers. In One Volume, 4to, muslin, gilt edges......................................$3.50
Turkey morocco super extra................................$5.50

THE HISTORICAL ESSAYS,

Published under the title of "Dix Ans D'Etude Historique," and Narratives of the Merovingian Era; or, Scenes in the Sixth Century. With an Autobiographical Preface. By AUGUSTUS THIERRY, Author of the "History of the Conquest of England by the Normans." 8vo., paper.......................... .$1 00
Cloth $1 25

BOOK OF THE SEASONS;

Or, The Calendar of Nature. By WILLIAM HOWITT. One Volume, 12mo, cloth.......................................$1
Calf extra..$2

PICKINGS FROM THE "PORTFOLIO OF THE REPORTER OF THE NEW ORLEANS PICAYUNE."

Comprising Sketches of the Eastern Yankee, the Western Hoosier, and such others as make up Society in the great Metropolis of the South. With Designs by DARLEY. 18mo., paper..50 cts.
Cloth..75 cts.

NOTES OF A TRAVELLER

On the Social and Political State of France, Prussia, Switzerland, Italy, and other parts of Europe, during the present Century. By Samuel Laing. In One Volume, 8vo., cloth.....$1.50

HISTORY OF THE CAPTIVITY OF NAPOLEON AT ST. HELENA.

By General Count Montholon, the Emperor's Companion in Exile and Testamentary Executor. One Volume, 8vo., cloth, $2.50 Half morocco...$3.00

MY SHOOTING BOX.

By Frank Forrester, (Henry Wm. Herbert, Esq.,) Author of "Warwick Woodlands," &c. With Illustrations, by Darley. One Volume, 12mo., cloth...75 cts. Paper covers..50 cts.

MYSTERIES OF THE BACKWOODS:

Or, Sketches of the South-west—including Character, Scenery, and Rural Sports. By T. B. Thorpe, Author of "Tom Owen, the Bee-Hunter," &c. Illustrated by Darley. 12mo, cloth, 75 cts. Paper... 50 cts.

NARRATIVE OF THE LATE EXPEDITION TO THE DEAD SEA.

From a Diary by one of the Party. Edited by Edward P. Montague. 12mo, cloth...$1

MY DREAMS:

A Collection of Poems. By Mrs. Louisa S. McCord. 12mo, boards ....75 cts

AMERICAN COMEDIES.

By James K. Paulding and Wm. Irving Paulding. One Volume, 16mo, boards..50 cts.

RAMBLES IN YUCATAN;

Or, Notes of Travel through the Peninsula: including a Visit to the Remarkable Ruins of Chi-chen, Kabah, Zayi, and Uxmal. With numerous Illustrations. By B. M. NORMAN. Seventh Edition. In One Volume, octavo, cloth.................................$2

THE AMERICAN IN PARIS.

By JOHN SANDERSON. A New Edition. In Two Volumes, 12mo, cloth..$1.50

This is the most animated, graceful, and intelligent sketch of French manners, or any other, that we have had for these twenty years.—*London Monthly Magazine.*

ROBINSON CRUSOE.

A Complete Edition, with Six Illustrations. One Volume, 8vo, paper covers..$1.00
Cloth, gilt edges...$1.25

•

SCENES IN THE ROCKY MOUNTAINS,

And in Oregon, California, New Mexico, Texas, and the Grand Prairies; or, Notes by the Way. By RUFUS B. SAGE. Second Edition. One Volume, 12mo, paper covers ....50 cts.
With a Map, bound in cloth..75 cts.

THE PUBLIC MEN OF THE REVOLUTION:

Including Events from the Peace of 1783 to the Peace of 1815. In a Series of Letters. By the late Hon. WM. SULLIVAN, LL. D. With a Biographical Sketch of the Author, by his son, JOHN T. S. SULLIVAN. With a Portrait. In One Volume, 8vo. cloth$2.50

ACHIEVEMENTS OF THE KNIGHTS OF MALTA.

By ALEXANDER SUTHERLAND. In One Volume, 16mo, cloth, $1.00
Paper...75 cts.

ATALANTIS.

A Poem. By WILLIAM GILMORE SIMMS. 12mo, boards, 50 cts.

LIVES OF MEN OF LETTERS AND SCIENCE.

By HENRY LORD BROUGHAM. Two Volumes, 12mo, cloth, $1.50
Paper $1.00

THE LIFE, LETTERS, AND JOURNALS OF LORD BYRON.

By THOMAS MOORE. Two Volumes, 12mo, cloth..............$2

THE BOWL OF PUNCH.

Illustrated by Numerous Plates. 12mo, paper............50 cts.

CHILDREN IN THE WOOD.

Illustrated by HARVEY. 12mo, cloth, gilt..................50 cts.
Paper ....25 cts.

TOWNSEND'S NARRATIVE OF THE BATTLE OF BRANDYWINE.

One Volume, 8vo, boards..$1.

THE POEMS OF C. P. CRANCH.

In One Volume, 12mo, boards............................37 cts.

THE WORKS OF BENJ. DISRAELI.

Two Volumes, 8vo, cloth $2
Paper covers...$1

NATURE DISPLAYED IN HER MODE OF TEACH-ING FRENCH.

By N. G. DUFIEF. Two Volumes, 8vo, boards..................$5

NATURE DISPLAYED IN HER MODE OF TEACH-ING SPANISH.

By N. G. DUFIEF. In Two Volumes, 8vo, boards..............$7

FRENCH AND ENGLISH DICTIONARY.

By N. G. Dufief. In One Volume, 8vo, sheep.................$5

FROISSART BALLADS AND OTHER POEMS.

By Philip Pendleton Cooke. In One Volume, 12mo, boards...50 cts.

THE LIFE OF RICHARD THE THIRD.

By Miss Halsted. In One Volume, 8vo, cloth...........$1.50

THE LIFE OF NAPOLEON BONAPARTE.

By William Hazlitt. In Three Volumes, 12mo, cloth......$3
Half calf..$4

TRAVELS IN GERMANY, BY W. HOWITT.
EYRE'S NARRATIVE.   BURNE'S CABOOL.

In One Volume, 8vo, cloth....................................$1.25

CAMPANIUS HOLMES'S ACCOUNT OF NEW SWEDEN.

8vo, boards..$1.50

IMAGE OF HIS FATHER.

By Mayhew. Complete in One Volume, 8vo, paper....25 cts.

SPECIMENS OF THE BRITISH CRITICS.

By Christopher North (Professor Wilson) 12mo, cloth. $1.00

A TOUR TO THE RIVER SAUGENAY, IN LOWER CANADA.

By Charles Lanman. In One Volume, 16mo, cloth....62 cts
Paper.. 50 cts

TRAVELS IN AUSTRIA, RUSSIA, SCOTLAND, ENGLAND AND WALES.

By J. G. Kohl.   One Volume, 8vo. cloth....................$1.25

LIFE OF OLIVER GOLDSMITH.

By James Prior.   In One Volume, 8vo, boards............... .2

OUR ARMY AT MONTEREY.

By T. B. Thorpe. 16mo, cloth......................................62 cts.
Paper covers...50 cts.

OUR ARMY ON THE RIO GRANDE.

By T. B. Thorpe. 16mo, cloth......................................62 cts.
Paper covers...50 cts.

LIFE OF LORENZO DE MEDICI.

By William Roscoe.   In Two Volumes, 8vo, cloth...........$3

MISCELLANEOUS ESSAYS OF SIR WALTER SCOTT.

In Three Volumes, 12mo, cloth...................................$3.50
Half morocco...$4.25

SERMON ON THE MOUNT.

Illuminated. Boards..$1.50 .
     "   Silk..$2.00
     "   Morocco super......................................$3.00

MISCELLANEOUS ESSAYS OF THE REV. SYDNEY SMITH.

In Three Volumes, 12mo, cloth...................................$3.50
Half morocco...$4.25

MRS. CAUDLE'S CURTAIN LECTURES..................12½ cts.

SERMONS BY THE REV. SYDNEY SMITH.

One Volume, 12mo, cloth...75 cts.

MISCELLANEOUS ESSAYS OF SIR JAMES STEPHEN.

One Volume, 12mo, cloth.......... ....$1.25

THREE HOURS; OR, THE VIGIL OF LOVE.

A Volume of Poems. By MRS. HALE. 18mo, boards.. 75 cts

TORLOGH O'BRIEN:

A Tale of the Wars of King James. 8vo, paper covers 12½ cts.
Illustrated...87½ cts.

AN AUTHOR'S MIND.

Edited by M. F. TUPPER. One Volume, 16mo, cloth....62 cts.
Paper covers...50 cts.

HISTORY OF THE ANGLO-SAXONS.

By SHARON TURNER. Two Volumes, 8vo, cloth...........$4.50

PROSE WORKS OF N. PARKER WILLIS.

In One Volume, 8vo, 800 pp., cloth, gilt......................$3.00
Cloth extra, gilt edges...$3.50
Library sheep..$3.50
Turkey morocco backs...$3.75
  "   extra...$5.50

MISCELLANEOUS ESSAYS OF PROF. WILSON.

Three Volumes, 12mo, cloth.......... ....$3.50

WORD TO WOMAN.

By CAROLINE FRY. 12mo, cloth................................60 cts.

WYATT'S HISTORY OF THE KINGS OF FRANCE.

Illustrated by 72 Portraits. One Volume, 16mo, cloth...$1.00
Cloth, extra gilt..$1.25

aned